CONTEMPORARY
WORSHIP MUSIC

CONTEMPORARY WORSHIP MUSIC

✤

A Biblical Defense

JOHN M. FRAME

P&R
PUBLISHING
P.O. BOX 817 • PHILLIPSBURG • NEW JERSEY 08865-0817

Printed in the United States of America

Composition by Colophon Typesetting

Library of Congress Cataloging-in-Publication Data

Frame, John M., 1939–
    Contemporary worship music : a biblical defense / John M. Frame.
      p. cm.
    Includes bibliographical references and indexes.
    ISBN 0-87552-212-2 (pbk.)
    1. Contemporary Christian music—History and criticism. 2. Church music.   I. Title.
    ML3187.5.F73   1997
    264′.2—dc21   97-22791

To the New Life Churches,
who swim against the current
of Reformed opinion
for the sake of
the Reformed gospel

Contents

Preface

After writing *Worship in Spirit and Truth* (WST), I became familiar with some spoken and written critiques of Contemporary Worship Music (hence, CWM) that I thought deserved answers. WST did contain three chapters on music in worship, but I felt that more needed to be said. The critiques of CWM were plausible on evangelical, particularly Reformed, premises, but they did not persuade me. Indeed, they seemed to me in the final analysis to be quite wrong-headed, and to be symptomatic of some deeper problems afflicting contemporary evangelical theology generally. The issue of CWM became, in my mind, a key to open up certain broader problems that Reformed theology will have to face if it is to present the gospel cogently in our time.

I thought at first that I could handle these problems briefly, perhaps even as an article, or as an appendix to WST. But the "broader issues" kept intruding on my thoughts. One question would lead to another, then to another. Every argument against CWM seemed like the tip of an iceberg. Clearly, I needed to treat these matters at length and with an approach not constricted by the adult Sunday school format of my previous book.

There will be some overlap here with the former book; my over-all approach to worship has not changed. But the main thrust of this volume is quite different. It deals, ostensibly, with a much narrower subject (CWM), but, at a deeper level, with relationships to much broader theological questions. The ideas here, if valid and persuasive, will have important ramifications for all our theological labors.

Thanks again to all who have guided my thinking in this area. A list of them is found in the preface to WST. In the preparation of this volume, I have been particularly grateful for interactions with (in alphabetical order) the Common Practice discussion group, Iain Duguid, W. Robert Godfrey, D. G. Hart, Stephen N. Hays, James B. Jordan, Reggie Kidd, Bruce McKechnic, George Miladin, Lois Swagerty, and Tom Ziegler. Many thanks to P&R Publishing, particularly Thom Notaro, for his work as editor, and Barbara Lerch, for her assistance.

Not everybody on this list of my helpers will like this book, but they will understand, I think, that I mean it as a constructive contribution to the dialogue. May God bless our common labor in these important matters.

CHAPTER 1

❧

Orientation

Time magazine recently noted that Christian Contemporary Music (CCM) is making a major impact upon the popular recording industry. More and more radio stations are adopting "religious music" formats, consisting largely of CCM. For twenty-five years, many churches have been using CCM worship songs (which I will call Contemporary Worship Music, or CWM).[1] Yet both CCM in general and CWM in particular have been quite controversial among Christian writers, especially those who deal with the theology of worship.

The Purpose of This Book

In this book I would like to try to sort out some of the issues surrounding CWM and to defend a limited use of it in Christian worship. In my view, some of the criticisms of CWM are valid up to a point; but they are usually overstated and not adequately balanced in relation to other legitimate considerations. When seen in proper perspective, these criticisms should keep us from naively accepting everything in the CWM literature. Certainly it would

1

not be right to abandon traditional hymnody entirely in favor of CWM. But CWM may, and should, in my judgment, play a significant role in the worship of the church.

I also intend to look closely at the assumptions and methods lying behind the current critiques of CWM. For as I indicated in the preface, I believe that these background questions have an importance beyond that of CWM. Some of those issues are

- the relation of Christ to culture,
- the relation of Scripture to tradition in theology,
- the relative priority of evangelism and nurture in the life of the church,
- the relation of divine sovereignty to human responsibility,
- the issue of contextualization (communicating in the language of our hearers),
- the relation of the intellect to the emotions,
- the place of aesthetic judgments in matters of worship,
- the nature of the Christian maturity we seek to encourage in worship,
- the nature of fairness in theological debate.

I fear that there is much confusion today on these matters among even the better evangelical theologians.

Where I Am Coming From

My position on CWM is bound to be controversial in the ecclesiastical and academic theological circles I inhabit. I am a Reformed[2] theologian, an enthusiastic subscriber to the Westminster Confession of Faith and the Larger and Shorter Catechisms. As a professor at Westminster Theological Seminary in California, I also subscribe to the "Three Forms of Unity" of the continental European Reformed churches: the Belgic Confession, the Heidelberg Catechism, and the Canons of Dordt. In these Reformed circles, there is very little sympathy among theologians, or even among popular writers, for CWM, though it has made some inroads into the worship of the churches.

The reader should understand, therefore, that my support of CWM has not been a reflex of my history. I have come to this position somewhat in defiance of my environment. I'm familiar with the arguments of confessional Protestants against the "dumbing down" of traditional worship caused by CWM. But I have not been persuaded. I believe that some of my confessional brothers and sisters have done injustice to CWM, and I hope in this volume to take some steps toward righting that wrong.

I also come to my position somewhat in defiance of my musical background. I took private lessons in classical piano for eight years; organ for five; clarinet for two; and harmony, counterpoint, and improvisation for three or four. In school I played in both band and orchestra, and in church sang in the choir. My mother wanted me to learn to play popular music as well, and I did take some lessons in that, too, for a while. But they never made much of an impact on me. I did enjoy the pieces, but my "popular" playing was always clunky, uninspired, inept. I sounded like an amateur classical musician trying to play popular pieces, and indeed that is what I was.

As a classical pianist and organist, I never came near to recital quality, but I did become a somewhat above average church musician. Given my other interests and limited talents, I probably could not have reached a higher level of performance. But, by God's providence, I have been able to use my musical training to serve the church.

Although I took no music courses in college, I continued to practice classical music. Grieg's A Minor Piano Concerto had been the apex of my piano studies in high school. After that I worked from time to time on concerti by Mozart, Schumann, Tchaikovsky, and Rachmaninoff, along with Beethoven sonatas and pieces by Bach, Chopin, Liszt, Brahms, Debussy, Ravel, and others. In my younger days, I would often spend one evening a week playing two-piano and four-hand pieces with a pianist friend or joining another friend in pieces for clarinet and piano. I have played over half of the organ works of Bach, my favorite composer, the complete organ works of Mendelssohn, Franck, and Brahms, and more recent music of composers such as Widor, Dupré,

Mulet, and Langlais. (My teacher was a student of Dupré, hence the emphasis on the French composers.) I have accompanied Handel's *Messiah* on a number of occasions, and other works such as Mendelssohn's *Elijah* and several Bach cantatas and motets. Most everywhere I have been, I have served as organist, pianist, and/or choir director in a local church. Until 1980, I worshiped exclusively in churches that were very traditional in their liturgical orientation. My serious exposure to CWM did not begin until age 41; I am now 58.

To this day I love classical music far more than any other musical genre, though I also enjoy at least occasional exposure to jazz and to older pop music. I don't have much of an ear for contemporary rock, and I don't like the moral and spiritual messages it tends to convey; hence we don't play it at home. I listen to classical CDs[3] and the local classical music station. I listen to CWM only to keep somewhat abreast of the movement, and to get ideas for songs to use in worship. CWM is not one of my personal musical passions.

I don't like to boast about my relatively small musical accomplishments, but I do want readers to know something of the background I bring to this study. Although I am not a professional musician, I don't think that I can fairly be regarded as a musical ignoramus or cultural Philistine. I believe that I know music at least as well as the average Reformed theologian. Nevertheless, I do think there is musical, as well as theological, value in CWM, and I will try in these pages to justify that appreciation.

So my views of CWM contradict what you might expect to hear from someone of my theological and musical background. But in a deeper sense, readers should not be so surprised. For one of the most important functions of scholarship, whether theological, musical, or whatever, is to rethink the conventional wisdom. We revere Luther and Calvin because they had the courage to rethink, from the ground up, the current traditions about salvation and worship. They were respectful of tradition, as all Christians should be. But they were not bound to it, only to the God of Scripture. In this volume, I hope, in a small way, to emulate their example.

What Is CWM?

In this section I will seek to define CWM descriptively, leaving evaluation to later points in the book. I know that description and evaluation cannot be completely separated. Some readers may think that this section amounts to positive evaluation simply because it fails to include criticism. But my goal here is primarily to achieve some common ground between critics and defenders of CWM. If we can agree on what we are talking about, then we can proceed more seriously to debate its merits. I fear that many critics of CWM base their criticisms on a few examples rather than on a thorough study of the music. I will seek to describe the broad shape of the genre, mentioning both points that are conducive to criticism and others that I shall find useful to my defense.

I shall define "CWM" fairly narrowly. The phrase will not serve to label all worship music that is both contemporary and Christian. Krzysztof Penderecki, for example, has written "esoteric church music" for our time, but his music is certainly not CWM.[4] Rather, CWM designates a particular movement in Christian music, which originated in California in the late 1960s.[5]

About that time, many young people from the sixties' counterculture professed to believe in Jesus. Convinced of the barrenness of a lifestyle based on drugs, free sex, and radical politics, "hippies" became "Jesus people." Doubtless there were many among them who looked on Jesus as just another "trip." But many became genuine disciples of the Lord.[6]

Historically speaking, awakenings of this kind typically bring changes to the church at large. Unfortunately,[7] they also tend to create new denominations, as they did in this case. Many joined the new "Calvary Chapels," founded by the Rev. Chuck Smith, which were particularly focused on reaching and teaching the youth culture. Others joined already-existing fellowships, sometimes by their very presence precipitating change in those bodies, changes of worship, music, and overall church life.

Revivals also tend to produce new outpourings of music. Many biblical references to music occur at spiritual high points in the history of God's people (see 1 Chron. 16; 2 Chron. 15; 23; 29; 35).

In church history, events such as the Protestant Reformation, the eighteenth- and nineteenth-century Awakenings, and modern crusade evangelism have all produced new forms of worship music. And the newly evangelized Jesus people of the 1960s produced CWM.

CWM is distributed by a number of publishers and record companies, such as Integrity's Hosanna! Music, Scripture in Song, Birdwing Music, and Mercy Publishing (connected with Vineyard Ministries). The largest publisher-recorder is Maranatha! Music, which grew out of the Calvary Chapel movement.[8] One can keep fairly abreast of CWM by listening to Maranatha's[9] series of "Praise" recordings and by looking through the *Maranatha! Music Praise Chorus Book* (hence, MMPCB)[10] which comes out in a new edition every four or five years. This volume serves, practically, as the CWM "canon" for many churches. It is also useful to listen to various CWM recording artists such as Michael Card, Amy Grant, the late Keith Green, Steve Green, Rich Mullins, Twila Paris, Sandi Patty, Michael W. Smith, John Michael Talbot, and James Ward.

Many CWM songs have words from Scripture. The Bible texts are often short, "snippets" as critics like to say. But there are longer texts as well, such as versions of the Lord's Prayer and shorter psalms in their entirety. Leonard Smith's "Our God Reigns"[11] paraphrases Isaiah 52:13–53:12, with some interpolations, as does James Ward's pair of songs, "Isaiah 53" and "He Shall Be Satisfied."[12] There are also versions of the Apostles' Creed, such as "This Is What I Believe" by Walt Harrah and John A. Schreiner,[13] and "In God the Father I Believe," by Frank de Vries, set to music by George Miladin.[14] Graham Kendrick's "We Believe" is not the Apostles' Creed, but it is very much a creedal summary of the gospel.[15]

In other songs, the words are extra-scriptural and nontraditional, but often very similar to the praises of the Psalms, such as "Great Is the Lord" by Michael W. Smith and Deborah S. Smith.[16] CWM songs are often called "Praise Songs" because praise is such a dominant theme of their texts. But the topical index of MMPCB indicates also calls to worship; songs of assurance; songs about the church or family of God; songs of comfort, commitment, communion, confession; and so on. I shall have more to say later on the variety of biblical themes reflected in CWM.

Most of the songs are one-stanza "choruses." Others contain several stanzas with only slight variations between them, such as "Father, I Adore You" by Terrye Coelho.[17] In this piece, the three stanzas are the same, except that the first word changes from "Father" to "Jesus" to "Spirit." However, there are also a number of songs in MMPCB that have several stanzas and that read much like traditional hymns. Many of these are by Graham Kendrick, such as his "The Servant King"[18] and "Shine, Jesus, Shine."[19]

The tunes and musical arrangements tend to reflect a popular style somewhat like the "soft rock" of the early 1970s.[20] It is this style which serves to define CWM in the minds of many, but it would be an exaggeration to say that CWM totally lacks stylistic variety. Even the "soft rock" style permits variation in tempo, major or minor mode, volume, melodic interest, harmonic possibilities, etc., at least as much as the more traditional styles of church music.

And CWM (defined, say, by the above-mentioned books and singers) is not always "soft rock." James Ward's music is deeply influenced by African-American gospel music (indeed, by many *kinds* of gospel, as he has pointed out). In MMPCB it is hard not to hear that influence in, for example, Bill Batstone's "Stand in the Congregation."[21] And we must not forget the Messianic Jewish music, popularized by the Liberated Wailing Wall and other Hebrew Christian singers, such as "Trees of the Field" by Stuart Dauermann and Steffi Karen Rubin.[22] That music is quite distinctive, with minor keys, yet joyful rhythms, the heritage of a long folk tradition—not at all fairly described by the phrase "soft rock."

MMPCB also contains country-western influenced music, such as the Gaithers' "Because He Lives,"[23] and "There's Something About That Name."[24] There are also older choruses like "I Will Sing of the Mercies,"[25] "This Is the Day,"[26] "Spirit of the Living God,"[27] and "His Name Is Wonderful."[28] And we should not ignore the fact that some of the songs are very reminiscent of traditional hymnody, such as Steven L. Fry's "Lift Up Your Heads."[29]

CWM is, therefore, not totally different from past traditions of church music. But it is not difficult to distinguish in a general way between CWM and the styles of music found in traditional hymnals: (1) CWM is far more contemporary and popular in its literary and musical idioms, rather than traditional or classical. (2) Most of it consists of one-stanza choruses as opposed to the multistanza poetry of traditional hymnody. (3) The texts of CWM tend to be far simpler than those of traditional hymnody. (4) In CWM there is far more emphasis on praise (as opposed to lament, confession of sin, teaching, personal testimony, or supplication) than in traditional hymnody, though other aspects of worship are also present.

CWM and Contemporary Worship

One of the problems in evaluating CWM is taking proper account of its relationship to the broader phenomenon of "Contemporary Worship" (CW). CW is generally understood to be a form of worship that is more "seeker-friendly" than traditional worship models, placing more emphasis on evangelism in worship. CW tends to avoid historic liturgies and old-fashioned language in order better to communicate with modern people.

I shall say more about CW in later chapters. Many critics of CWM deal with it as a mere aspect of CW in writings that concern CW generally rather than CWM in particular. In my opinion that is an inadequate analysis. CWM originated in a particular historical context of revival. It is not the product of someone's strategy to make worship more contemporary. Indeed, I think that CWM songs can fit well into worship services that are structured along traditional lines; you can have CWM without CW.

Nevertheless, for many people CWM stands or falls with CW. And they are right to the extent that CWM seems to fit *best* into a style of worship in which all the elements, not only the music, speak the language of today. I had hoped that I could deal with CWM independently of CW, without getting into the debates surrounding the latter. But the more I read and think about the subject, the more that hope seems impossible. So in this book I will have some things to say about CW, mostly in its defense. I hope the reader will understand, however, that CW is not the *main* concern of this volume, and I don't pretend here to deal adequately with all of the issues surrounding CW. But questions about CWM are regularly intertwined with questions about CW, and so I am reconciled to some level of engagement with the CW controversy.

Notes

1. In my original draft of this book, I called what I was defending CCM. But several readers thought that was much too broad, even though I made plain that I was not defending the use of *all* CCM in worship. "CCM" refers to everything from Christian heavy metal to Maranatha praise choruses, including much that nobody, not even the CCM artists, would recommend for use in worship. And so, I learned, the use of "CCM" would mislead knowledgeable readers. I thought about using the standard phrase "Praise and Worship" (P&W), but I resisted that. This phrase is redundant, since praise is, after all, part of worship. So I have settled on CWM.

2. In my view, "evangelical" is a broad category embracing many more specific ones, such as Lutheran, charismatic, dispensational, fundamentalist, and Reformed. My concern in this book is specifically with Reformed theology, my own tradition, but also with evangelical theology, the broader tradition to which I adhere. I will therefore describe my position either as "evangelical" or as "Reformed," as is appropriate to the context.

3. Mostly the above-named composers and recent church choral music. I do have certain "guilty pleasures" such as Delius and Grainger.

4. Marva Dawn, *Reaching Out Without Dumbing Down* (Grand Rapids: Eerdmans, 1995), 167. Dawn also cites an unpublished paper of Thomas Gieschen, which presents a taxonomy of ten different kinds of contemporary worship music.

5. There were other factors, too, in the origin and development of CWM, such as (1) the use of "testimonial music through the leadership of Bill Gaither in the early sixties" (Robert Webber, "Enter His Courts with Praise," in *Reformed Worship* 20 [June 1991], 9), (2) the "body life" movement of the 1970s (Ray Stedman, *Body Life* [Ventura, Calif.: Regal, 1972]), (3) the charismatic movement, in which worship styles hitherto distinctive to Pentecostalism were introduced into churches of other traditions. To put the matter in broader perspective: since the Protestant Reformers insisted on congregational singing in the vernacular languages, there has been movement in the churches toward greater congregational participation, less formal structure, more contemporary language, and more popular styles of music. In every generation there has, therefore, been some conflict between advocates of the old and of the new. See my *Worship in Spirit and Truth* (Phillipsburg: P&R Publishing, 1996), chap. 10.

6. Some of my correspondents have urged me to be more critical of this movement since it was not, of course, characterized by the distinctives of Reformed theology. Some, on this ground, even question whether it was a genuine work of God. I do think that the Jesus people would have been better off had they been taught Reformed theology from the beginning. Nevertheless, in this book I take it as a given that God does work outside the channels of my own tradition. (For some argument to this effect, see my *Evangelical Reunion* [Grand Rapids: Baker, 1991].) And after seventeen years of living in California and coming to know many of those converted in the 1970s revival, I have no doubt that God was working through that movement. Among many of these people there remains to this day a great love for God's Word and for the gospel of God's grace in Jesus Christ.

7. I have argued in *Evangelical Reunion* that denominations are a result of sin, either on the part of existing denominations, or on the part of those forming new denominations, or both. Many otherwise friendly critics have taken my position to be extreme, but I am unmoved. I challenge them to find any scriptural justification for the formation of new denominations. There is *one* church in the New Testament, which Christ bought with his own blood (Acts 20:28), founded on the apostles and prophets (Eph. 2:20), governed by elders whom believers must obey (Heb. 13:17). How could anyone, apart from sin, have dared to found an alternative to that glorious body of Christ?

8. Maranatha! is now part of Word Publishing Company.

9. Or is it "Maranatha!'s"? One hardly knows what to do with exclamation marks attached to words. It is interesting to deal with an industry in which Hosanna! competes with Maranatha!

10. I shall be referring to the Third Edition (in red), published in 1993.

11. MMPCB, 219.

12. In *James Ward His Songs* (Bryn Mawr, Pa.: Celebration Press, 1975), 57–60, 54–56.

13. MMPCB, 22.

14. In the *Trinity Hymnal*, rev. ed. (Atlanta and Philadelphia: Great Commission Publications, 1990), no. 741. But is this CWM? Given its atypical musical style, it is hard to say. There are a number of gray areas in the distinction between what I'm calling CWM and other kinds of contemporary worship music.

15. MMPCB, 65. Other creedal settings worthy of note (thanks to Reggie Kidd): Wes King's "I Believe," Amy Grant's "We Believe in God," Rich Mullins's "Creed." The latter is a studio piece, on Mullins's CD, "Liturgy, Legacy, and a Ragamuffin Band," perhaps not really practical for congregational use, but memorable in many ways.

16. Ibid., 11.

17. Ibid., 151.

18. Ibid., 150.

19. Ibid., 2. Over the last ten years there has been a "rediscovery of hymns" in CWM publications and recordings. Maranatha's *100 Hymns, 100 Choruses* (Nashville: Distributed by the Benson Company, 1987) includes songs of both genres, with suggestions for medleys including both. Several recent CDs and tapes from Maranatha! and Hosanna! have included traditional hymns. Occasionally these are arranged with a more CWM style; but sometimes they are presented with pipe organ sounds or other traditional settings.

20. Dawn, *Reaching Out*, 167.

21. MMPCB, 313.

22. Ibid., 103.

23. Ibid., 20.

24. Ibid., 233.

25. Ibid., 66.

26. Ibid., 210.

27. Ibid., 277.

28. Ibid., 108.

29. Ibid., 153.

CHAPTER 2

⤫

A Theology of Worship: Some Basics

In this chapter as in the last, I am primarily seeking to define common ground between the critics and the defenders of CWM, although here the common ground may not be as extensive. I do believe that thoughtful Christians on all sides of this issue share some basic convictions on the nature of worship. I have expounded a theology of worship at some length in my *Worship in Spirit and Truth*. The present treatment will overlap that book somewhat, but in summary fashion, and with an eye to the specific concerns of this volume.

God's Transcendence and Immanence

Worship is the priestly labor of acknowledging the greatness of our covenant Lord. We worship to honor him, not ourselves. Thus we adore his wonderful power, holiness, and love. And we respond in gratefulness for his salvation in Christ. We recognize ourselves as his creatures in his image, his servants by nature. And we confess that we are lost, guilty sinners apart from grace. We find in him our only source of forgiveness and eternal blessing. So Christian worship is God-centered and Christ-centered.

In discussions of worship, therefore, it is especially important that we understand who God is and how he is related to us. God is, first of all, the *Lord,* the Ruler and Creator of all things, who controls the entire course of nature and history (Eph. 1:11). As such, he is *transcendent,* exalted over all his works, deserving the utmost in adoration and praise. God's transcendence is a theme that pervades the Psalms, as in Psalm 99:1–3:

> The LORD reigns,
>   let the nations tremble;
> he sits enthroned between the cherubim,
>   let the earth shake.
> Great is the LORD in Zion;
>   he is exalted over all the nations.
> Let them praise your great and awesome name—
>   he is holy.

At the same time, God is *immanent,* near to all his creatures. God's immanence does not contradict his transcendence; rather his transcendence *implies* immanence. Since God perfectly knows and controls all things, he is intimately involved in everything that happens in the creation. Nothing happens without his knowledge and power. Nobody can escape from him. He is everywhere (Ps. 139; Heb. 4:12–13).

Not only is God transcendent and immanent in relation to the creation in general. He is also transcendent and immanent in a special way to his believing people. He is *their* Lord, who redeems them from slavery and sin and calls them to new lives of obedient love to him (Ex. 20:2; Deut. 6:4–9). The Lord is their King (Ps. 99:1), transcendent in his rule over them. He is also immanent: their Savior and Deliverer (Isa. 43:11), the Lord *with* his people (Ex. 3:12; 25:8). He is their God and they are his people (Rev. 21:3).[1]

In worship, we acknowledge God's transcendent greatness in reverence and awe (Heb. 12:28), in praise and adoration, in humble recognition of our need for his forgiveness (Isa. 6:5). We also recognize God's immanence, rejoicing that he has chosen to draw near to us, particularly in Christ. Through Jesus, he is our Lord, and also our Father (Matt. 6:9), Friend (John 15:15), and Brother (Heb. 2:11–12). In worship, God is present in a special way so that even an unbeliever may sometimes recognize it (1 Cor. 14:25). God draws near to us, and we also draw near to him (Ps. 73:28; Heb. 12:22–24). Away from worship, we long to be near him in this way (Ps. 84:1–4).

A biblically balanced view of worship must take into account both God's transcendence and his immanence, his exaltation and his nearness, his majestic holiness and his unmeasurable love. This balance is not always easy to maintain. Churches that focus on divine transcendence are in danger of making God appear distant, aloof, unfriendly, unloving, devoid of grace. Churches that focus on God's immanence sometimes lose sight of his majesty and purity, his hatred of sin, and the consequent seriousness of any divine-human encounter. To maintain this balance, we must go back again and again to the Scriptures themselves so that we may please God in worship rather than merely acting on our own intuitions.

Some critics of CWM find it difficult, I think, to accept a fully scriptural view of God's immanence. Note the following passage from Michael S. Horton:

> As we have seen, the "theology of glory" characteristic of Gnosticism and mysticism in general, has as its goal the ascent into the presence of God to touch him and to see him in all of his glory, even though he has said that no one can see him and live. "Draw me closer, Lord," goes another Vineyard song. "Draw me closer, dear Lord, so that I might touch You . . ." This is an invitation to disaster, for apart from Christ (who is nowhere to be found in this song) "our God is a consuming fire," and to see him or touch him is to be turned to ash (Heb. 12:29).[2]

Certainly, to say the least, Horton is missing some biblical nuances here. There is certainly a sense in which God draws near to believers and we draw near to him (Pss. 69:18; 73:28; 119:151; 148:14; Jer. 30:21). In that nearness, believers do behold the beauty of God, his glory (Pss. 27:4; 63:2; 97:6; John 11:40; 17:24). We seek more of the beauty of God's dwelling places (Ps. 84). By the blood of Christ, we have boldness to enter into the holiest place (Heb. 10:19), a place that struck terror into the hearts of Old Testament believers.

It is true that apart from grace we cannot see God's face and live. Horton evidently believes that Contemporary Worship and CWM make little reference to the grace of Christ, by which we rightly draw near to God. I hope to persuade readers in this book that in fact CWM is Christ-centered, though, like the Psalms, not every CWM song refers specifically to the atonement. But Horton's broad polemic against the language of drawing near to God in worship is quite unscriptural. Better to sing with the psalmist, "But as for me, it is good to be near God" (73:28).

God-Centered Worship

Because God is who he is, worship must be God-centered. We worship God because he supremely deserves it, and because he desires it. We go to worship to please him, not ourselves. In that sense, worship is *vertical,* focused on God. We should not go to worship to be entertained, or to increase our self-esteem, but to honor our Lord who made and redeemed us.

This is not to deny, however, that worship brings benefits to the worshipers. The benefits to the church can be summarized in terms like "edification," "strengthening," and "upbuilding" (see 1 Cor. 14:26 in different translations). There are also benefits to unbelieving visitors: conviction of sin and an encounter with the presence of God (1 Cor. 14:24–25). In these ways, worship has a *horizontal,* as well as a vertical, dimension.

There is no contradiction between the vertical and the horizontal, between the God-centeredness of worship and the benefits available to the worshipers. For it is that very God-centeredness that blesses us. Meditating on God's greatness and his saving work in Christ is what enables us to grow in our devotion and obedience and thus to experience more and more the blessing of God in our lives. The horizontal dimension of worship, therefore, does not open the door wide to anything that happens to please the worshipers.

The Rules for Worship

It should therefore be apparent that worship is directed by God himself, through his Word in Scripture. In worship as in all of life, God's Word must take precedence over any of our own creative ideas. In planning worship, we want above all to know what pleases God; and only the Scriptures give us clear indication of what God wants us to do in his presence. Therefore, the Protestant Reformers, particularly Calvin and his followers, emphasized *sola Scriptura* as the chief rule of worship. What we do in worship must be warranted by Scripture.

There are also positive things to be said about church tradition, about which various traditions differ! At least we should say that God gives teachers to the church (Eph. 4:11) and calls us to submit to them (Heb. 13:7, 17). This exhortation, surely, pertains not only to teachers presently living but also to those through whom God has guided the church through its history. Through such passages we should come to a generally positive view of church tradition.

On the other hand, Protestants deny that tradition is infallible. Historically they have insisted on a sharp distinction between the words of God and the words of men; and they have placed church tradition (synods, councils, theologians) in the latter category. Scripture alone is in the former sphere, God's inspired, inerrant Word (2 Tim. 3:16–17). Hence, Scripture is "sufficient" (*sola Scriptura*) to provide the ultimate standards for faith and life. Scripture itself contains a polemic against those who would worship according to human rules rather than the Word of God (Isa. 29:13; Matt. 15:8–9).

Human Creativity in Worship

Is there, then, no room in worship for human planning or creativity? Certainly there is an important role for these. Scripture's own principles are always to some extent general. God leaves us to work out the specifics by our own Spirit-led wisdom, within the broader principles of the Word. Scripture tells us to pray together, for example, but it does not tell us precisely what prayers to utter in a given worship service. We make that decision, seeking to abide by the general biblical teachings concerning prayer. God governs worship by his commands, but we are responsible to *apply* those commands to our particular circumstances.[3]

Music is certainly one of the areas in which God seeks to use the creative abilities of his people. Scripture does not prescribe the use of any particular tunes for hymns, or of any particular musical style. Of course, we may reasonably conclude from biblical premises that music used in worship should be of good quality, appropriate to the texts employed, and meaningful to the worshipers. There may also be other guidelines in Scripture relevant to our choice of music. But we must make the specific decisions ourselves within those limitations.

Communication

Much of the worship leader's creative task is seeking effective means of communication. God, of course, understands our thoughts before we express them, and so communicating with him is not a problem. But there are problems of communication on the horizontal axis. We have seen that worship ought to be edifying to the church and meaningful even to outsiders. Edification and meaningfulness require attention to language. Therefore, the apostle Paul in 1 Corinthians 14 insists that worship be intelligible: it should not be conducted in unknown tongues unless those tongues are interpreted.

Paul does not say here that everything in worship must be perfectly and immediately understandable to everybody. According to verse 35, some aspects of worship led women in the Corinthian church to ask questions during the meeting. Paul commands them to save their questions for their husbands at home, rather than demanding immediate answers in the worship service itself. In this case, the apostle does not place the congregation's understanding above all other considerations; the Corinthian women will have to be content for a time with less than perfect comprehension. Nevertheless, it is clear that throughout the chapter (which is the only extended discussion in the Bible of New Testament worship services), Paul places a high priority on the clarity, the intelligibility, of the language used in worship. Similarly, the Protestant Reformers insisted that worship be conducted in the vernacular languages rather than in Latin.

Therefore it would certainly be unscriptural to say that since worship is directed toward God, it doesn't matter whether the worshipers understand it or not. We do not glorify God if we fail to communicate on the human level.

Nor would it be scriptural to say that since God is sovereign in communicating his grace, it is irrelevant whether or not our worship is intelligible. To say that is to place the sovereignty of God in opposition to human responsibility. But in the Bible, God gathers his elect through the work of human preachers (Matt. 28:19–20; Rom. 10:14–15). God's sovereign work is accomplished partly through human actions. Certainly preaching must be intelligible; all churches assume that when they require ministerial candidates to take courses in homiletics. No one ever makes the argument that since God is sovereign, it doesn't matter whether our preaching is clear, logical, or exegetically sound. Though God can save people through poor preaching, such preaching is, nevertheless, undesirable. To the extent that it fails to set forth the truth of Christ clearly, cogently, persuasively, and powerfully, it is not preaching of God's Word.

If preaching should be intelligible, the same must be said of worship in general, as Paul emphasizes in 1 Corinthians 14. Singing is a form of teaching in Colossians 3:16, the response of those who have let the Word of Christ dwell in them richly, in all wisdom. God teaches us in our songs, but we also teach one another, joining divine sovereignty to human responsibility. Just as unintelligible preaching is, to that extent, not preaching of God's Word, so unintelligible language and music in worship is, to the extent that it fails to edify, not true worship. Worship I don't understand is not worship from my heart; it is not *my* worship of God.[4]

Now, intelligibility, to some extent, implies contemporaneity. This is not to say that everything must be perfectly up-to-date. The occasional use of archaic language can be effective communication. Archaisms, if they are not used all the time, can arrest the attention and elicit a thoughtful hearing, if only by arousing healthy curiosity about the meaning of the language. Ancient language can also convey to worshipers a sense of unity with the church of past centuries, and that is a good thing. Most Americans today can understand the English of the King James Version of Scripture up to a point, and its eloquence is often moving.

But most congregations today have departed from King James English, and for good reason. That form of English is a barrier to communication if it is the predominant language of worship.

As with language, not all music is equally understandable to all people. Music hugely appreciated in some circles—whether by Palestrina, Hindemith, J. S. Bach, or Michael W. Smith—will leave some listeners cold. Music that leaves you cold does not enhance the communication of the gospel to you.

When music leaves someone cold, it is not necessarily the fault of the composer or the performer. There are many reasons why music can fail to communicate, and often the problem is with the listener. Listeners often lack the education to appreciate a particular style of music. Or they may lack the cultural background: one major reason for racial and ethnic segregation in the churches, I believe, is the inability of various cultural groups to appreciate one another's music. We might wish that the church could take time to give every member a musical and ethno-musical education, but in view of everything else God calls the church to do, that wish may be unrealistic.

Sometimes music leaves us cold because of our own sin. When we come to worship with hard hearts, seeking at most something that will give pleasure to us or reinforce our own self-righteousness, the worship music, whatever the style, often fails to speak to us.

One kind of sin relevant to our study is musical snobbery. Sometimes music leaves us cold because we are too stubborn to open ourselves to a style different from what we are used to. Snobs are of many types: high art lovers who cannot bear to hear anything from mere popular culture, but also "with-it" modern types who look down on others for being less than fully up-to-date. Such snobbery is, more evidently than the problem of a lack of education, one that God has called his church to deal with. But the church must also reckon with the fact that while we are on this earth, we are imperfectly sanctified. And until we all develop a perfect openness to everybody else's music, how shall we worship?

Or the problem may be with the music itself: a particular kind of music may be inappropriate for worship, or even associated with worldliness. The church must often decide what is appropriate or not, and there are hard cases here. Sometimes it is hard to draw the line between a legitimate concern for appropriateness and the kinds of aesthetic snobbery noted above.

In any case, the church should seek music that does not leave its congregation cold—music that enhances its praises, preaching, and prayers; music that really edifies the people. That music should be contemporary at least in the sense of being meaningful to modern people, in the sense of not leaving most of them cold. It should leave them with the sense that the Word of God has been made more vivid, more memorable, not less, by the music. To some congregations, the chorales of Bach will be fully contemporary in this sense. But I do believe that most congregations will find worship more intelligible if they sing and hear *some* music of our own time.

The Great Commission

After his resurrection and before his ascension into heaven, Jesus left these words to his disciples:

> All authority in heaven and on earth has been given to me. Therefore go and make disciples of all nations, baptizing them in the name of the Father and of the Son and of the Holy Spirit, and teaching them to obey everything I have commanded you. And surely I am with you always, to the very end of the age. (Matt. 28:18–20)

This "Great Commission" defines the task of the church in the world until Jesus returns. Here Jesus, on the basis of his comprehensive authority (v. 18) and promised presence (v. 20), commands and empowers the church to disciple all nations. The discipling work involves both evangelism and nurture: both the work of baptizing new converts and the work of teaching them to obey the whole Word of God.

As we have seen, worship has both a vertical and a horizontal focus. It seeks to glorify God and to edify the congregation. These are not, of course, separate from one another, since God is glorified in the edification of his people, and since people are edified only in learning how better to glorify God. The horizontal focus is defined by the Great Commission. In worship, we evangelize, baptize, and teach.

There is a lot of controversy today about the relation of evangelism and nurture in worship. Should the worship of the church be geared primarily toward the seeker,[5] or should it be primarily a gathering of the people of God, who then *depart* from worship to evangelize non-Christians? Some writers are quite dogmatic in saying that there is no place at all for evangelism in worship.[6] On the contrary, I believe that some emphasis on evangelism is appropriate to biblical worship.

The New Testament does present the regular worship meeting as primarily a believers' service. Plainly in 1 Corinthians 14, the vast majority of those attending worship are Christian. The non-Christian visitor is an anomaly (1 Cor. 14:24–25). And the apostle Paul, in letters read to the congregations during worship, does not hesitate to address them as "saints" (Rom. 1:7; 1 Cor. 1:2; 2 Cor. 1:1; etc.).

Nevertheless, the New Testament does not exclude non-Christians from the worshiping assembly. And it does encourage the church (1 Cor. 14:24–25) to plan its worship with the unbelieving visitor in mind. The point is not that the church should compromise its gospel to please unchurched visitors; quite the contrary. It should proclaim the fullness of God's Word with the utmost clarity, forcefulness, and offensiveness.[7] What could be a better testimony to the unbeliever than the sight and sound of

God's people praising their Lord for their salvation in Christ and announcing God's judgments on the wicked?

The idea that we should give no attention to evangelism in the weekly worship except to send God's people out to do their own witnessing is contrary to the biblical doctrine of the church. That idea is essentially individualistic. In Scripture, rather, evangelism is the corporate work of the church (as well as, of course, the work of individual Christians). The Great Commission mandates it to the church as a body. Therefore, the church should be mobilized for evangelism; it should be seen as, among other things, an evangelistic organization, seeking to bring the gospel to its community and beyond. With evangelism so central to the church's divine calling, everything the church does will have an evangelistic aspect, including Sunday worship. When we meet to worship God on Sunday, we cannot forget that we are Christ's ambassadors to a lost world; rather at that time we must be reminded all the more of our divine commission.

Therefore, a focus on evangelism in worship is essential to the nurture of believers. Believers need continual reminders of the nature of the church's task, particularly since it is so easy for a church to become ingrown. Evangelism and nurture, therefore, are not neatly separable.[8]

Furthermore, there is nothing scripturally wrong with holding meetings (other than the weekly worship) that are specifically evangelistic and seek to meet the unbeliever where he is. The apostle Paul spoke in synagogues, lecture halls, and outdoors; surely we may do the same. And there is no reason why a church building cannot be used to hold such public meetings. Even at these meetings, we must observe scriptural standards. There is to be no compromise of the message, and worship at these meetings must observe biblical norms. But in such meetings there should obviously be special efforts, even beyond those of the stated worship services, to speak and sing the language of the streets. Like Paul, we must, without compromising the gospel, "become all things to all men so that by all possible means I may save some" (1 Cor. 9:26).

Becoming all things to all men is often costly and humbling. It means putting aside our preferences for the sake of our audience.

This includes our preferences in music. In evangelistic meetings, and to some extent even in corporate worship (granted its evangelistic aspect), we must be willing sometimes, and to some extent, to set aside our musical traditions so that the Word may sound clearly to the non-Christian.

I am not saying that we must set aside all of our traditions, all the time. Not everything we do in worship must be simplistic and modern, or easily accessible to unbelievers. God's people need to hear the depth of God's Word, and to some extent that is beneficial to the non-Christian visitor as well. It is good for the seeker to know that there are riches in God's truth far beyond his present grasp, riches treasured by Christians through the centuries, that he will never appreciate unless by God's grace he adopts a whole new way of thinking. But in every service there must be some words, some music, that directly challenge his unbelief, words and music that in a plain and vivid way point the visitor to the justice and the love of Christ.

The Unity and Variety of the Church

Jesus established one church, not many (Matt. 18:18–19), and he prayed that the church would always be one, even as he and the Father are one (John 17:11, 21–23).[9] It is tempting to say that because Jesus' prayers are always answered, the church as we know it today must in fact be one in every respect relevant to Jesus' prayer. On this view, Jesus must not have been praying for the church's organizational unity, because if he had been, his prayer went unanswered. He must have had in mind unity in some vaguely defined "spiritual" sense.

But this argument misses a fundamental point. Godly prayers, including those of Jesus, are always answered, but not right away. Indeed, some of the Father's own expressed desires, such as for the judgment of the wicked and the eternal bliss of the righteous, are achieved not immediately but after a period of time. Jesus' prayers, therefore, provide us with direction for the future, not merely a description of the status quo. His prayer for unity, therefore, includes unity in every respect commended in

God's Word: organizational, doctrinal, familial, and the vital unity of mutual love.

Therefore, the New Testament recognizes the brokenness of the church through time and seeks to remedy that, as in Paul's critique of factionalism in 1 Corinthians 1–3. As I said in chapter 1, denominationalism is factionalism writ large; it is not God's will for his people.[10] And the New Testament presents love as that which distinguishes believers from the world (John 13:34–35; 15:12; 1 John 3:10–11; 4:7–21).

The unity of the church is a unity in diversity. Church unity is all the more remarkable, all the more difficult to achieve, because it is a unity joining a wide variety of people, differing in ethnic background, language, gender, gifts, and ages (see Gal. 3:28; Rom. 12; 1 Cor. 12; Eph. 4:1–16).

Biblical worship takes both the unity and the variety of the church into account. It displays our unity by bringing us all together. In worship we praise God with one voice, confess the same truth, hear the same Word, receive the same sacraments. We recognize one Lord, one faith, one baptism.

Worship also exhibits the variety of the church. In the Psalms there are simple songs (such as 23; 100; 131; 133) and very complicated ones (such as 68 or 119). Some Scripture texts tell stories that children can follow easily. Others raise deep concepts like Trinity and predestination that humble the greatest minds.

In New Testament worship, many voices are heard (1 Cor. 14:26), many suggestions made. The complexity of worship under these conditions challenges the church's leaders to maintain order. It is also difficult, amid such diversity, to maintain love within the body. In a congregation of rich and poor, the rich are always tempted to neglect the poor or to push them aside in worship (1 Cor. 11:20–22; James 2:1–7). Those temptations must be resisted. Love goes against our sinful grain.

We should conclude that in music as in every other area we must seek to love one another, honoring the diversity of the body to protect its unity. As we have seen, diversity presents problems of musical communication. But we can now see that problem as at least in part a problem of love. When sophisticated members of the church insist that worship employ only the most sophisticated music of their own culture, what has happened to their love for those who are poorly educated or of a different cultural stream? Or, from the opposite side of our musical wars: when advocates of contemporaneity want to set the traditions of the church completely aside and replace them with something largely meaningless to the older generation, are they acting in love? Are they honoring their spiritual fathers and mothers?

The responsibilities of love are reciprocal, according to Ephesians 5:22–6:9. Wives are to submit to their husbands, but husbands are to love their wives. Children must obey their parents, but parents should not anger their children. Slaves should obey their masters, but masters should not threaten their slaves. In the church, the great musical generation gap should also be addressed with loving mutual deference. The younger should submit to the older (1 Peter 5:5), but, like wise parents, the older should not provoke the younger to anger. The elders of the church are not to lord it over God's people, but, like Christ, to be their servants (Matt. 20:20–26; 1 Peter 5:1–4). All are to seek not only their own interests but those of others (Phil. 2:3, note context).

How do we love one another and defer to one another in the selection of church music? First, we must constantly search our hearts for evidence of selfishness. Are we seeking to have it our own way or to serve our brothers and sisters? Forsaking selfishness means seeking to honor the preferences of others as much as we can. Yes, we must also consider questions of quality and appropriateness, as I plan to do later in this book. But we should be aware of our tendency to confuse those questions with questions of taste. And we should resolve that if anyone in the church is to be offended over a mere matter of taste, it should be us rather than someone else.

Therefore, unless it can be shown to be inappropriate for worship, everyone's music should be heard: old people's and young people's music; European, African American, and other ethnic music; complex music and simple music. This is how we defer to one another—serve one another—in the body of Jesus Christ.

The Nature of Nurture

The previous section exhorts us to accept one another as we are, and to bend to one another's needs and desires, as much as we can within biblical norms. But the Great Commission calls us not to remain as we are: not to be stagnant, but to grow in our worship of God. We are to teach, and be taught, all that Jesus has commanded us. So worship should encourage growth in grace. It should challenge worshipers to increase in their knowledge of God's Word, in their obedience, in their love of his presence in worship. And as they grow in their knowledge of Scripture, that increased knowledge should be reflected in the hymns they sing, the prayers they offer, and the level of teaching they desire.

It might seem, then, that when a congregation is rightly growing in God's grace, it will concurrently move from relatively simple worship to relatively complex, from elementary to profound, from lower to higher intellectual levels. There is some truth in that principle, but it is very misleading unless balanced by the following qualifications:

1. A church that takes seriously the Great Commission will expect always to have at its worship services, not only mature and maturing believers, but also new and young believers (to say nothing of unchurched visitors), who must begin at the beginning of the quest for maturity. So if simple songs are for the immature, there should always be some simple songs.

2. But simple songs are not only for the immature. Consider Psalms 23, 117, 131, and 133, which, though short and relatively simple, contain teaching that any serious Christian must recognize as profound. Indeed, any song that is really scriptural in content will be profound in this way. The Lord Jesus taught us that we should be as little children (Matt. 18:3; 19:14). The Christian gospel is a relatively simple message (John 3:16; 1 Cor. 15:1–4), with profound implications. Those who sneer at the message of grace, seeking something supposedly more profound, crave "the wisdom of this world," as Paul describes it (1 Cor. 1:20). But the gospel that Paul presented without eloquence or

pretense of learning (1 Cor. 2:1–4) was the power of God for salvation to those who believed (Rom. 1:16). Being saved by such a gospel message, we should not look down in pride upon its expression in simple songs.

Surely, complex and difficult ideas, whether spoken and sung, have an essential place in the church. Psalms like 68 and 88, the books of Job and Ecclesiastes, and New Testament passages like Romans 9 and Revelation 4–22 teach us so. There is a place in the Christian life to ponder complexities. But there is also a place in the lives even of the most mature Christians to ponder the profundity of the simple.

3. Part of the process of Christian maturity is a growth in love for the less mature, in the deference described in the previous section of this chapter. My point is not that mature Christians should indulge all the wants of the less mature. Elders of the church, for example, may rightly include in worship songs and spoken language not immediately accessible to younger Christians, (a) for the benefit of older Christians, (b) to challenge the younger to advance in their understanding, and (c) to teach the younger the virtue of honoring others, especially their fathers and mothers in Christ. But to be mature is not to demand one's own way. And often, what is best for the church as a whole is to hear and sing the gospel in simple terms.

4. Since the Great Commission defines the church's task, one important part of nurture is to expose young Christians to the work of evangelism. It is wrong, therefore, to oppose "nurture" and "evangelism," as we are sometimes tempted to do. When worship reaches out to the lost, believers learn some of their most important lessons.

So it is not only the narrowly evangelistic side of the Great Commission that calls us, sometimes, at least, to contextualize the worship of the church in intelligible, contemporary, and sometimes simple language. The nurture of believers, the maturing of babes into soldiers of Christ, often requires the same thing. These considerations should be taken seriously even by those who completely reject any evangelistic emphasis in the regular worship of the church.

Conclusion

Based on theological considerations fairly widely accepted in Christian churches, I believe we have seen several important reasons at least to consider the use of new music in worship.

1. God's transcendence does not exclude, but rather implies, his nearness to his creation, and especially to his worshiping people.
2. The God-centeredness of worship does not exclude, but requires, consideration of the worshiper. Although God does not need contemporaneity to play his role in the worship meeting, human worshipers do.
3. In determining the rules for worship, we should recognize that *sola Scriptura* requires of us a willingness to examine critically even the most revered human traditions.
4. Music is an area in which we have little explicit scriptural direction, and in which, therefore, human creativity should be encouraged, within the limits of general biblical standards.
5. Communication is important in worship, and intelligible communication must be contemporary at least in the sense of being understandable to modern ears.
6. The Great Commission requires us to speak, to some extent, the verbal and musical languages of people outside the church.
7. Maintaining unity among the diversity of the church's membership requires that we defer to one another in love, being willing to sing one another's music rather than insisting on the music we most enjoy.
8. The singing of simple, contemporary songs plays a role not only in evangelism but also in the nurture of God's people.

Notes

1. For a more extended discussion of God's lordship and how it implies his transcendence and immanence, see my *Doctrine of the Knowledge of God* (Phillipsburg, N.J.: Presbyterian and Reformed, 1987), especially 11–61.

2. Michael S. Horton, *In the Face of God* (Dallas: Word, 1996), 200.

3. This discussion summarizes my own view of the Presbyterian "regulative principle for worship" set forth in more detail in *Worship in Spirit and Truth* (Phillipsburg, N.J.: P&R Publishing, 1996). Not all Presbyterians agree with me on this matter. Nevertheless, I will not discuss that controversy here. A stronger view of the regulative principle will not much affect one's view of CWM. Nobody believes that Scripture gives us specific instruction as to what type of music to use in worship. Even those who believe in the exclusive use of the Psalms in worship must still decide whether or not to use CWM versions of the Psalms. So our present question is not resolved even by the most restrictive form of the regulative principle, though it is true that people who hold conservative views of the regulative principle usually *tend* to prefer more traditional forms of musical expression.

4. Ralph Gore makes the point well: "The worship we present must, after all, be *our* worship—*our* offering of praise to God. Worship is never an abstraction, but is always the concrete work of some body of believers. If we would practice faithfulness in worship, we must understand the twin horizons of God's unchanging word and the rapidly changing culture in which we live." In "Warming Up the Frozen Chosen," *Faith and Practice* 2:1, 43.

5. In this book, I use the term "seekers" as it is typically used in the Church Growth literature, for any unchurched person with an interest in Christianity. Theologically it is important to keep two principles in view: (1) Apart from grace, nobody seeks God from the heart (Rom. 3:11), though many unbelievers express some interest in religion. (2) God's grace works invisibly, like the wind (John 3:8); so we cannot know when it begins to lead someone to true faith in Christ.

6. D. G. Hart, in "Reforming Worship," *Touchstone* 8:4 (Fall, 1995), 19, notes as a principle of Reformed theology that *"worship is theocentric"* and then concludes, "This means that worship is not designed for evangelism. The fact that services on the Lord's Day have become 'seeker sensitive' shows a perversion of the nature of worship." I hope on these pages to offer a perspective that is more biblically balanced.

7. I am, of course, talking about the offensiveness of God's Word itself, not that which may be caused by our own sinful behavior.

8. An excellent presentation of this concern is C. John Miller, *Outgrowing the Ingrown Church* (Grand Rapids: Zondervan, 1986).

9. On this point and others in this section, see my *Evangelical Reunion* (Grand Rapids: Baker, 1991, now out of print) for further discussion.

10. In *Evangelical Reunion,* of course, there is much discussion of balancing considerations. I do not advocate simply leaving existing denominations or seeking a "lowest common denominator" fellowship. In the present context, that would only be another kind of divisiveness. My point here is that we need to learn from the sad history of denominational division so as not to repeat the mistakes that created that division. It is therefore important that we learn to work together in worship despite the potentially divisive controversies that have arisen.

CHAPTER 3

❧

Some Obvious Virtues of CWM

At each stage of my argument there are, perhaps, more and more readers who are unpersuaded. But I am sincere in saying that even in this chapter, as in the first two, I am trying to establish common ground between defenders and critics of CWM. It does seem to me that before we even speak of the most controversial aspects of the question, those on all sides *should* agree that there are a few *obviously* good things about CWM.

This chapter will not impress the type of critic who attacks his opponents in a scorched-earth fashion, taking no prisoners. There are, of course, critics like that in every field, those who cannot bring themselves to admit even a smidgen of virtue or truth in the objects of their attack. That sort of criticism can be rhetorically impressive, but it usually loses credibility on analysis. It is highly improbable that anyone is wrong all the time. Even a stopped clock, after all, is right twice a day. Reformed doctrine does teach the total depravity of the race; but it also teaches that even the most wicked among us display to some extent the influence of God's common grace, so that nobody is as bad as he could be.[1]

The best wake-up call to the scorched-earth critic is for him to become a victim of the same tactics. As one who has been the object of such critical reviews, I can testify that they seem much more cogent when directed against others than when directed against oneself.

So I am offering the critics an opportunity to make their criticism much more cogent and persuasive by making a few minor concessions at the outset. They should begin their argument with, "Of course, we must recognize that CWM does have a certain freshness," etc. That sort of admission suggests, at least, that the critic has done a bit of thinking about these issues and is not merely parroting a party line. It may even imply that the critic actually has some familiarity with CWM, whether or not that impression is true.

So in this chapter I want to mention some things about CWM that I think, granted the theological premises of chapter 2, are obviously good. Critics can employ these as concessions to enhance their initial credibility; defenders can use them to begin their defense. In the next chapter I will allow the tables to be turned on me: I will accept the burden of reviewing the critics' case as sympathetically as I can, trying to understand and appreciate the genuinely valid points they have made.

God-Centeredness

The first thing to be said is that CWM is profoundly God-centered and therefore Christ-centered. The first hymn in MMPCB, by Dave Moody, reads

> All hail, King Jesus! All hail Emmanuel,
> King of kings, Lord of lords, Bright Morning Star.
> And throughout eternity I'll sing your praises,
> And I'll reign with You throughout eternity.

This is praise to God in Christ. That theme of adoration pervades MMPCB and CWM generally. Hence these hymns are often called "praise songs."

The proportion of songs in CWM devoted primarily to praise

is far greater, I would judge, than the proportion in traditional hymnody. That is not a criticism of traditional hymnody, for there are purposes for music in worship other than that of focused praise (purposes like teaching, supplicating, meditating, lamenting, etc.) But as a matter of fact, CWM is, more than most genres, devoted to the adoration of God. It is therefore, in an obvious sense, God-centered, and we should recognize that.

This fact is all the more surprising because CWM is youth music. Young people have the reputation of being self-preoccupied and self-indulgent, and certainly those traits have often appeared in the history of Christian youth music. I went through adolescence during the ascendancy of Young Life and Youth For Christ. We sang songs like "Do, Lord" and "Arky Arky." I don't condemn those songs in every setting, but I can understand why some regard them as self-centered entertainment. But the youth music coming out of the 1970s was a different thing entirely:

> Be exalted, O God, above the heavens,
> Let Thy glory be over all the earth.[2]

This generation of youth had learned to praise! They expressed awe and wonder at the majesty of God. They honored his attributes and his mighty acts. They prayed for God's purposes, his honor, and his glory to prevail on earth as in heaven.

One would think that critics devoted to fairness and committed to the theological standard of God-centered worship would take at least some pleasure in this remarkable fact. But instead, critics of CWM, with little if any hesitation, regularly identify CWM with what Christopher Lasch called "the culture of narcissism."[3] I find that approach quite unjustifiable, and I find it hard to believe that critics of this sort have given more than superficial attention to the texts of the music.

Scripturality

CWM is also, for the most part, scriptural, and strikingly so. Of course all good hymnody is scriptural in the sense of communicating biblical teaching. But CWM is typically scriptural in another sense as well, that of being literally close to the biblical text itself. In CWM we hear actual biblical language, over and over again.

I do not believe that all worship music must reproduce biblical phrases and cadences. Song in worship is an *application* of God's Word, not a mere repetition of it.[4] It is therefore legitimate for song in worship to use words, phrasings, and cadences different from those of Scripture itself. Nevertheless, it is a good thing for God's people to get those words, phrasings, and cadences into their hearts. Helping Christians to do so is one (though not the only) legitimate goal of church music.

Many CWM songs are simple repetitions of biblical texts or combinations of Scripture texts on the same or complementary themes. Others are combinations of biblical texts with responses by the worshipers, such as "A Shield About Me" by Donn Thomas and Charles Williams,[5] which cites Psalm 28:7 and then responds with repetitions and hallelujahs.

Still others use extra biblical words. But a surprising proportion of these extra-biblical texts speak biblical language; they sound like the Bible. Consider "Great Is the Lord" by Michael W. and Deborah D. Smith:[6]

> Great is the Lord, He is holy and just,
> By His power we trust in His love.
> Great is the Lord, He is faithful and true,
> By his mercy He proves He is love.
>
> Great is the Lord, and worthy of glory.
> Great is the Lord, and worthy of praise.
> Great is the Lord, now lift up your voice,
> Now lift up your voice:
> Great is the Lord! Great is the Lord!

The phrase "Great is the Lord" is found in 48:1, but the song is not, of course, a setting or paraphrase of Psalm 48. Nevertheless, it uses the Psalter's language of praise.

Again, I am constrained, with some amazement, to compare

this to the music of my youth. Although it is still fun to sit around with a group of kids and sing "I've got the joy, joy, joy, joy, down in my heart," I must confess that there is a vast difference between that and "Great is the Lord." CWM is not only scriptural in its doctrine, but it teaches congregations the verbal and conceptual patterns of the Psalter itself, using tunes that are memorable and vivid to contemporary worshipers. Is that not something we can all applaud?

Indeed, although CWM is both defended and criticized for being "modern" (even "postmodern," as we shall see!), there is something very archaic about its use of biblical phraseology. Who would have dreamed thirty years ago that kids with guitars would one day take delight in singing phrases like "Lord, I Lift Your Name On High"?[7] Archaic, and profound too, despite all the talk about how CWM "dumbs down" Christian worship. "Lifting up God's name" (as, for example, in the Hebrew text of Ex. 20:7, or, in a different connection, in Ps. 34:3) is an idea with rich biblical associations that has rarely been appreciated by the Christian church. But now we are hearing it from kids with guitars and synthesizers. Out of the mouths of babes, God is ordaining praise. They are leading us into something ancient and theologically deep. Isn't there something remarkable about that, for which we should be thanking God and thanking these young hymnwriters?

Our congregation sings a song based on Revelation 15:3–4:

> Great and marvelous are your works, Lord God almighty,
> Just and true are your ways, King of the ages.
> Who will not fear you, O Lord,
> And bring glory to your name,
> For you alone are holy.
> All nations will come and worship before you,
> For your righteous acts have been revealed. [Hallelujahs][8]

The tune is stately, then lively, a D minor "Jewish-type" song. The melody, harmony, and rhythm are musically intriguing—more so, I would say, than most traditional hymnody. Through it our people have come to know and love this Scripture text, which gives us confidence that God's righteousness will be vindicated in the eyes of all nations of the earth. Were it not for this modern song arrangement, I'm sure that this text would not be part of our spiritual arsenal. But because of CWM, it is in our hearts, a powerful sword of the Spirit. Again, CWM has led us into something scriptural, ancient, profound, comforting, and challenging. Should we not thank God for CWM?

I grant, of course, that not all CWM is on the same level. There are also songs like William Gaither's "There's Something About That Name,"[9] which never quite gets around to telling us what the "something" is. It does list several names of Christ, and it does affirm that "kings and kingdoms will all pass away," presumably in contrast with the kingdom of Jesus which remains forever. That is worthwhile. I think we can thank CWM, among other things, for bringing to the church's attention afresh the rich and biblical concept of God's "name" and his "names." CWM songs move us to sing about "Elohim," "Adonai," "El Shaddai," "Yeshua," "Wonderful Counselor" and so on, and to meditate on the nuances of these. That is edifying, and the Gaither song might be used to introduce or summarize that teaching. But the term "something" spoils it: that word leaves a big conceptual blank to be filled in by the worshipers' too-active imaginations. And it plays too great a role in the song to be replaced by, well, something else.

True enough, but traditional hymnody, too, is not all on the same level. In every genre, we must use discernment. I do believe that there is a higher percentage of good hymns in the traditional literature, almost by definition. What we call "traditional hymns" are hymns that have been tested by time. CWM must also be tested in order to become part of that tradition. Much of it will not be heard thirty years from now. But some of it will be tested and survive that test. And certainly, as long as God's Spirit remains with his church, the *spirit* of CWM, that of meditation on the very words and concepts of Scripture, will continue.

Why is it that in this area critics don't give CWM its due? The usual criticism is that although CWM songs use Scripture, they don't use enough of it. The portions are too small: "snippets" or "smatterings." There is not enough context. And they limit their subject matter narrowly to praise rather than including also the wider content of the Psalter and of Scripture as a whole—lament, supplication, imprecation, complaint.[10]

Some replies:

(1) Such criticism assumes that the more Scripture literally included in a song, the better. But among those who reject the position of exclusive psalmody,[11] none of us actually makes this assumption. Many of the great traditional hymns do not include any literal Scripture references at all, although great hymns always present biblical doctrine.

(2) No song can say everything Scripture says. (Nor, of course, can a sermon, or even a systematic theology.) In that sense, all songs taken from Scripture are "snippets." The real question is how much context we must include in order to avoid distorting the biblical message. Mature Christians do differ on that sort of question. It must, however, be answered in the concrete. Let's ask it about "How Majestic Is Your Name" by Michael W. Smith.

> O Lord, our Lord, how majestic is Your name in all the
>   earth.
> O Lord, our Lord, how majestic is your name in all the
>   earth.
> O Lord, we praise Your name.
> O Lord, we magnify Your name,
> Prince of Peace, mighty God,
> O Lord God Almighty.[12]

This song uses Psalm 8:1, but no other verses of the psalm. It follows verse 1 with some praise language that is not found in Psalm 8 but is typical of other biblical songs of praise.

Should we say that this song is unacceptable because it uses verse 1 without the following context? I think not. The song is a perfectly good song of praise. Even if it were not based on any Scripture text at all, it would be worth singing. The fact that it contains one verse from Psalm 8 should be a plus rather than a minus.

In some cases a lack of context may indeed falsify the meaning of a particular text used in a song, but I think those cases are rare, so rare that I have failed in my attempt to find an actual example to include here.

(3) This criticism doesn't fit well with those mentioned in the first section of this chapter. One cannot say that CWM is narcissistic and then turn around and say that CWM is too focused on praise as opposed to laments and sorrows.

(4) But, granted the legitimacy of singing laments as well as praises, how is a congregation to learn the broader content of the Psalter and of Scripture as a whole? How can they sing laments, supplications, complaints? Well, by singing other songs. "How Majestic Is Your Name," good as it is as a song of praise, will not meet every need of the worshiping congregation. There are CWM songs that recognize the dark side of God's providence. Our congregation, for example, sings a version of Habakkuk 3:17–18:

> Though the fig tree shall not blossom,
> And there be no fruit on the vine,
> Though the fruit of the olive shall fail,
> And the fields produce no food,
> Though the flock should be cut off from the fold
> And there be no cattle in the stall,
> Yet I will rejoice in the Lord,
> Yet I will rejoice in the Lord,
> Yet I will rejoice in the God of my salvation.[13]

We also sing a song by Bob Smith based on Psalm 73:25–26:

> Whom have I in heaven but you, O Lord?
> And on earth there is none I desire but you.
> My heart and my flesh, they shall fail me,
> But God is my strength, the strength of my heart,
> My portion forever,
> My portion forever.[14]

And we sing Danny Daniels's "I Will Trust in You,"[15] and Jamie Owens-Collins's "The Battle Belongs to the Lord."[16] We love

"Job's Song,"[17] by my friend the Rev. Andrew John Noch, which reads, in part,

> Take my faith and make it strong, Lord.
> Take my hope and make it rise.
> Take my wealth and make me poor, Lord.
> Take my soul until it cries:
> Praise and honor all to thee,
> As I fall on bended knee,
> I will sing eternally
> To you, my king!

There are more CWM songs about trials and persecutions than most critics suppose. There is a whole sub-genre of CWM dealing with "spiritual warfare." Maranatha! Records has a "spiritual warfare series." One CD called "The Battle Belongs to the Lord" includes, together with the title song, "Jesus, Mighty God" (". . . and every foe will tremble at your name"),[18] "Victory Song/Call to War," and others. I have read some criticisms of CWM, which I cannot now locate, to the effect that the spiritual warfare songs are dark, harsh, militant, and so on. But, of course, so are the Psalms. And to criticize the spiritual warfare songs as too dark is at the same time to refute the charge that CWM is all sweetness and light.

But we should remember that God has not limited the church to using CWM exclusively! If there are not enough CWM songs about the dark side of life, why not turn to other traditions? Why should we not use CWM songs of praise (with the few darker songs) and also use traditional hymns like William Cowper's "God Moves in a Mysterious Way," and "Sometimes a Light Surprises"? It is true, and a legitimate criticism, to say that CWM does not cover all areas of biblical teaching equally well. But we should not conclude from that observation that CWM is, in general, an unworthy medium of worship.

(5) As I mentioned in chapter 1, some CWM songs present whole psalms and other longer passages of Scripture. So not all CWM Scripture settings are "mere snippets."

(6) In worship it is valuable to use Scripture in many different ways. There is value in singing entire psalms, though few churches actually sing the longer ones all the way through. And there are also advantages in singing smaller passages. Longer Scripture settings cover larger areas of doctrinal and emotional territory. Shorter ones give believers the opportunity to meditate on one or two crucial verses or ideas in some depth. CWM usually (not always) takes the latter alternative. But rather than criticizing it on that account, we ought to be thankful for the opportunity it presents.

When thinking about the use of Scripture in worship, we are tempted to think in quantitative terms: CWM uses "less" Scripture than many Scripture settings of traditional hymnody. I do think that our worship ought to give broad coverage to biblical texts and ideas. CWM does not, certainly, in itself give sufficiently broad coverage to sustain all aspects of evangelical worship over many years. Thus I advocate the use of both CWM and traditional hymns.

But we should think in qualitative terms as well as quantitative. When a congregation sings twelve stanzas of a psalm version to a traditional tune, they cover a large quantity of material, and that can be a good thing. But how much of it do they remember? How much of it has grabbed their imagination? How much of it will come to mind when they wake up the next morning? How much of it will return to comfort and challenge them in the midst of temptation or oppression? Surely there is also much to be said for the use in song of shorter portions of Scripture, set to unforgettable tunes, like "Great and Marvelous," which I mentioned earlier.

What I advocate is not either-or, but both-and. But those who condemn CWM because it doesn't itself offer broad enough coverage of biblical material often miss one of the really important *virtues* of CWM—that it gets its small portions of the Word of God into people's hearts. Perhaps as it matures, CWM will become more quantitatively comprehensive. But the fact that it has not attained such maturity should not prevent us from using it in those areas where it is already exceptionally edifying.

Freshness and Communication

The next virtues of CWM that I will mention are perhaps the most obvious. Most everyone grants that CWM has a contemporary, fresh feel to it. And most everybody grants that freshness is something good. Marva Dawn comments, "I hope churches will continually utilize fresh words and music to praise God . . ."[19] and later she commends contemporary worship for "rejecting tradition that has grown stale."[20] She doesn't, however, quite endorse CWM on this ground.

She should, however. This is certainly one of the major advantages in using CWM.

I will, however, qualify my judgment somewhat. Frankly, there is a certain monotony about CWM that detracts from the overall freshness of the style. I once subscribed to the monthly tape service of one CWM publisher, but I canceled that subscription after a year or so. After a while, the songs all sounded the same to me.

Part of the problem may be with me. As I said earlier, my love is classical music, not soft rock. And even with the classics I often have to hear a piece many times before I really start to like it. I don't have the time to listen to CWM tapes ten or fifteen times. When a friend suggests a new song, I will, however, listen to that song many times and play it over and over on the piano. So most of the songs I use in worship are songs suggested by other people whose opinions I respect.

Some of the monotony, however, is probably due to the style and genre; at least many knowledgeable musicians and liturgists think so, and I have no quarrel with them on that score. But, trying to see the matter in some perspective, my considered judgment is that although many CWM songs are interchangeable and uninteresting, there are some, indeed a large number, that are very striking, that just reach out and grab you (and that even grab me after four or five hearings). I have tried to use some of these as positive examples in this book.

These songs tend to communicate especially vividly with young Christians and unchurched visitors, and, as I said in chapter 2, communication to those groups is biblically important. There should also be concerted efforts to challenge mature believers, and CWM is less useful for that purpose, though not entirely irrelevant as we have seen. But as I emphasized in chapter 2, different groups in the church ought to defer to one another. There should be songs for the young and songs for the old, songs for the mature and for the less mature (children, particularly, should never be neglected in liturgy!), songs for the different culture-groups represented in the congregation, as well as songs that communicate well with everybody. Again, my suggestion is both-and, not either-or.

Notes

1. Compare my discussion of Cornelius Van Til's doctrines of antithesis and common grace in *Cornelius Van Til: An Analysis of His Thought* (Phillipsburg, N.J.: Presbyterian and Reformed, 1995), 187–230. Pages 241–309 and 339–86 also expound, in effect, a Christian ethic of criticism.

2. From "Be Exalted, O God," by Brent Chambers, in MMPCB, 25.

3. See Christopher Lasch, *The Culture of Narcissism: American Life in an Age of Diminishing Expectations* (New York: W. W. Norton, 1979). There are many references to this book in Marva Dawn's critique of modern evangelical worship (including CWM), *Reaching Out Without Dumbing Down* (Grand Rapids: Eerdmans, 1995), as in David Wells's two books, *No Place for Truth, or Whatever Happened to Evangelical Theology?* (Grand Rapids: Eerdmans, 1993), and *God in the Wasteland: The Reality of Truth in a World of Fading Dreams* (Grand Rapids: Eerdmans, 1994), chief sources of Dawn's critique. For Marva Dawn's critique of the narcissism of CWM and my response, see appendix 1.

4. I have criticized the position that only Psalm settings should be used in worship in my *Worship in Spirit and Truth* (Phillipsburg, N.J.: P&R Publishing, 1996), chap. 11.

5. MMPCB, 23.

6. Ibid., 11.

7. By Rick Founds, in MMPCB, 199.

8. I haven't been able to locate the source of this song. I learned it from hearing others sing it. I suspect it is unpublished, but I could be wrong.

9. MMPCB, 233.

10. See Dawn, *Reaching Out*, 89–90, and her quotation from Brueggemann on 89.

11. See note 4, above.

12. MMPCB, 217. Note here as we mentioned earlier the emphasis on praising the "name" of God.

13. Again, I lack information on authorship and publication data. There is a setting of this text by Tony Hopkins in *Scripture in Song,* vol. 2 (Nashville: Benson, 1981), 48, but that is not the one our congregation uses.

14. Unpublished so far, to my knowledge.

15. MMPCB, 315.

16. Ibid., 268.

17. So far unpublished.

18. "Jesus, Mighty God," by Rick Founds, in MMPCB 33.

19. Dawn, *Reaching Out,* 87.

20. Ibid., 93.

CHAPTER 4

⌘

The Case Against *CWM*

In the previous chapter I sketched, in very general terms, a positive case for the use of CWM in worship. In that discussion I tried to stick to the obvious, making points that in my view even the opponents of CWM should be willing to concede, though of course not all of them do. In that chapter I did refer to some criticisms of CWM, but mainly for the purpose of bringing out more clearly what I believe is good, right, and true about the songs. There I asked skeptical readers for a time to suspend their disbelief, to try to follow my argument sympathetically, if only to have a better understanding of how those on our side really think.

In this chapter, I turn the tables on myself. Still trying to build up common ground, I want to look at the critics' case as sympathetically as I can, to try to understand what really bothers them about the use of CWM in worship. For the most part, I have much respect for these critics. As the reader may gather from my earlier autobiographical remarks, I might easily have become a critic myself. My love of Reformed theology and of classical music has enabled me to walk quite a way in the footsteps of those who shun CWM. Indeed, I feel the way the critics do about many CWM songs, and I have been turned off by some "contemporary" worship services. Nevertheless, after considering all the objections, I still advocate some use of CWM in worship.

In this chapter, I will attempt to outline a comprehensive critique of CWM. I shall reply to that critique chiefly in later chapters, rather than this one, although I shall not be fastidious here about concealing my point of view. The criticisms mentioned here are taken from different writers. Each writer has a somewhat different slant, somewhat different concerns. None presents all the arguments that I shall list. But all deserve our thoughtful attention, and it is important for us to assess the cumulative argument that results from all the individual considerations mentioned in the literature.

A Historical Perspective

The case against CWM is rooted in deeper questions than "What shall we sing this Sunday?" or "What is a good hymn to use with a sermon on Romans 8?" Though not all critical writers go as far below the surface as I shall describe, it is important to consider their concerns in the context of a kind of identity crisis within contemporary evangelicalism.[1]

The term *evangelical* has been applied since the sixteenth century to Christians who emphasize "the personal appropriation of salvation and the spiritual importance of the reading of Scripture."[2] The term originally applied to writers within the Catholic church. But in the mid 1540s, "church authorities had become convinced that to be an *evangelical* was to be a *Lutheran*—and hence to be anti-Catholic."[3] For some years, then, *evangelical* and *Protestant* were virtual synonyms. In the eighteenth century, however, the movements of theological liberalism, on the one hand, and the Great Awakening, on the other, provoked further differentiation. Those who accepted the revival of the church under Wesley, Whitefield, and others, and who rejected the radical biblical criticism of the theological liberals, became particularly known as evangelicals, although the broader use of the term did not completely vanish.

As generally understood in present-day America (to which I will largely restrict my attention in this book) evangelicalism includes not only traditional Lutherans and Calvinists, but also Christians of Wesleyan, Anabaptist, and Pietist backgrounds and those influenced by dispensational or charismatic theology. Within these broad categories, of course, there are numerous subdivisions, combinations, innovations, and distinctives.

Evangelicalism began as a movement of real intellectual substance that powerfully influenced many aspects of Western culture. But lately it has fallen on hard times. Liberal biblical criticism and evolutionary science have rendered evangelical confidence in Scripture intellectually suspect among mainstream academics. Challenged on these and other issues, many evangelicals, especially during the early twentieth century, retreated from the academic and social mainstream, seeking to protect themselves and their children from unbelief rather than to engage in an intellectual and cultural offensive. Dispensational theology, which promised the imminent return of Christ, depleted the traditional evangelical emphasis upon long-term social reconstruction. The evangelicals entered the "world" to evangelize individuals, but not to influence social institutions or ideologies. An anti-intellectual, anti-academic spirit developed among them. During this era, evangelicals were often called *fundamentalists*, a term that took on connotations of anti-intellectualism and cultural separatism.[4]

Still more recently, according to many critics of the movement, evangelicals have allowed the pervasive secularism of the general culture to enter the church,[5] to the extent that there is confusion among them even concerning the fundamental gospel of salvation. Supposedly evangelical preachers have presented Jesus as the key to our earthly health and wealth rather than as the One who taught us to lay up treasures in heaven. Many purported evangelists have had little or nothing to say about Jesus as the mighty Lord of heaven and earth, who saves his people from their sins by his sovereign grace.

Thoughtful evangelicals have tried to re-establish within the movement sound doctrine, high intellectual standards, social conscience, and a stance that challenges modern secularism rather than succumbing to it. In David Wells's influential analysis, modern secular culture has influenced evangelical churches particularly in the following ways:

1. *Subjectivism:* basing one's life upon human experience rather than upon objective truth.[6]

2. *Humanism:* a man-centered life-and-world view in which God, even when confessed, makes little practical difference. Or, what is virtually the same, redefining God so as to eliminate any concept of his sovereignty. Imaginatively creating a God who exists to meet human needs, a "user friendly" deity.[7]

3. *Anti-intellectualism:* appeal to feelings rather than to intellectual understanding. A "dumbing down," which compromises a proper emphasis on sound doctrine and Christian maturity.[8]

4. *Psychologism:* psychological therapy as the way to deal with the most fundamental human needs.[9]

5. *Professionalism:* preoccupation with business management and marketing techniques as the model for achieving any kind of common enterprise.[10]

6. *Consumerism:* the notion that in all fields of endeavor we must have the goal of giving people what they want or what they can be induced to buy.[11]

7. *Pragmatism:* the view that results are the ultimate justification for any idea or action.[12]

8. *Temporal Chauvinism:* My term for Wells's concern that modern people tend to regard their time as superior to all past times, holding the belief that the present is always better than the past and the future will necessarily be better than the present.[13]

The effects of this mentality on the church, according to Wells, have been entirely detrimental. ("This book is insistently antimodern," he says.[14]) Because of the influence of modernity, theology no longer rules in the church.[15] Therefore God himself becomes unimportant, "weightless," in Wells's memorable term.[16] Although the church believes in God's existence, his existence makes no difference to the church's practical decision-making. God becomes "user friendly," not the holy, transcendent, awesome God of Scripture.

Therefore, says Wells, theology no longer governs the church in any meaningful way.[17] Sermons seek to set forth not God's Word but baptized equivalents of the latest cultural preoccupations ("felt needs"): psychic well-being, success in marriage, etc.[18] Theories of church growth and the practice of "mega-churches" substitute management and marketing theory for biblical principle, viewing congregations the same way businesses regard consumers of their products. So churches cater to the wants of people rather than to their true spiritual needs. Seminaries aspire to become professional schools, training ministers in these worldly values and skills.[19]

Contemporary Worship

I will not try to define "contemporary worship"[20] (CW) in any precise way, but I shall attempt a description. Usually, CW describes efforts to modify traditional styles of worship in order better to communicate with contemporary people. These nontraditional forms of worship have displayed fairly common patterns: more contemporary language and music, informal atmosphere, greater emphasis on joyful celebration, less on mourning over sin. The church seeks to encourage an atmosphere of welcome and friendliness. CW avoids "turn-offs" like ancient liturgy, emphasis on denominational history and theological distinctives, ten-minute prayers, forty-minute sermons, uncomfortable seats, ministers' begging for money, and crowded parking lots and rest rooms. The preaching assumes little congregational knowledge of Scripture and doctrine, and avoids technical theological language. It begins by addressing "felt needs." Sometimes the church uses drama, films, and multi-media, usually to pose questions that the sermon seeks to answer. In general, CW seeks to meet unchurched visitors where they are: to speak their language, and thereby lead them toward a commitment to Christ. CW is often called "seeker-sensitive" or "user-friendly," because it tries to be aware of where visitors are coming from more than has been the case in traditional worship.

There are many differences among churches that aspire to be seeker-sensitive. Not all of them go as far as what I have described above. Some use both traditional and contemporary hymns and even elements of traditional liturgy. Some put a considerable emphasis on sin, repentance, and grace. In the church where I serve, we have described ourselves as "seeker-sensitive, but not seeker-driven."

Some churches do not consider their seeker-sensitive meetings to be in the category of "worship." They regard these meetings, even though held on Sunday morning, as evangelism, and they hold services at other times of the week for actual worship. But other churches believe that they can combine evangelism and believers' worship at one service.

The Critique of Contemporary Worship

To the writers mentioned in the first section of this chapter, CW is symptomatic of the ills of the modern evangelical church. In terms of the eight categories listed earlier:

1. *Subjectivism:* CW, they argue, is too "subjective," rather than "objective": centered on the worshiper, his or her feelings and experiences, rather than on God.

2. *Humanism:* In CW, God himself becomes "user-friendly," rather than the transcendent, awesome, sovereign Lord of biblical revelation. Worshipers receive the impression that they can manipulate God or use him for their own purposes. At worst, CW is heresy, downplaying biblical teachings about divine law and human sin, leaving us with a gospel void of atonement and forgiveness.

3. *Anti-intellectualism:* CW is at best milk for babes, excluding anything that would nurture and challenge mature believers.

4. *Psychologism:* CW plays along with the psychological preoccupation of modern culture, offering quasi-psychiatric therapy to meet the felt needs of the audience, rather than the gospel of divine grace and the forgiveness of sins.

5. *Professionalism:* CW sees Christianity, even Christ himself, as a "product," to be marketed like any other. Thus it demeans Jesus and misleads its hearers as to his transcendent greatness.

6. *Consumerism:* CW therefore aims to give people what they want and think they need, rather than to rebuke their self-

prescriptions and confront them with God's estimate of their true need. As in the secular economy, consumerism tends to diminish real quality in music, architecture, liturgical language. Bad worship drives out good, as the churches aim at a "lowest common denominator" of worshipers. Thus worship becomes entertainment, the ultimate consumer commodity.

7. *Pragmatism:* CW seeks worldly goals, such as big churches, fame, and fortune, and it does whatever it can to draw people in, without asking what pleases God in worship.

8. *Temporal Chauvinism:* CW tends to be anti-traditional, particularly in its defense of itself as up-to-date and with-it. Advocates of CW have been known to attack traditional worship as dull, boring, old-fashioned, and otherwise unworthy of the attention of contemporary people. Opponents of CW, however, tend to be advocates of tradition, urging a recovery of roots.

Contemporary Worship and CWM

The current critique of CWM begins with the critique of CW. CWM is an inseparable part of CW, we are told, and what is wrong with CW is also wrong with CWM. I have mentioned eight areas of concern about CW. Note now how those areas relate to CWM.

1. *Subjectivism:* We saw in chapter 3 that some critics fault CWM with being preoccupied with the worshiper rather than with God.[21] Critics of CWM have the impression that this music does not do justice to the fact that salvation is "outside" us. As Michael Horton puts it,

> Biblical Christianity is concerned with what happened outside us, two thousand years ago, outside the city of Jerusalem. It is an "over there" religion, not an "in here" religion. It is centered on what happened externally, not on what happens internally.[22]

2. *Humanism:* The critics are concerned that CWM does not set forth the sovereign Lord of Scripture, but rather praises a god

made to the specifications of human beings, who exists to meet human need. Recall the complaints mentioned in chapter 3 concerning the alleged man-centeredness of CWM.[23]

3. *Anti-intellectualism:* As we have seen, CWM tends to be simpler than traditional hymnody, and in contemporary language. Therefore it makes fewer intellectual demands on the worshiper. It does not presuppose high levels of education, a love for high art, or theological sophistication. In the minds of critics, this simplicity reflects the anti-intellectualism, which they find in CW generally—a "dumbing down" of Christian worship.

4. *Psychologism:* Much of the appeal of CWM is in the emotions it elicits: ecstatic joy, with clapping and shouting, feelings of closeness (sometimes romantic, in the critics' estimation) with other worshipers and with Jesus, and so on. There are therapeutic overtones in all of this.

5. *Professionalism:* In ways suggested above, CWM strikes some observers as manipulative, as one technique for getting people to come to church and keep coming. It has been used in churches that have grown big; therefore it is recommended for all churches that want to become big, or bigger. It is one way of "managing" salvation and "marketing" the gospel. Such techniques replace God's sovereignty as the way of reaching the hearts of people.

6. *Consumerism:* CWM seems to be a way of giving people what they want, rather than what they ought to have. The church's standards are lowered to the level of pop culture, for that is where the church's product can find a market. Quality is a secondary, or even nonexistent, consideration. Because entertainment is almost the ultimate consumer commodity, CWM turns praise into entertainment. And, since entertainment is dominated by the entertainment industry, CWM then comes under the control of Christian music companies, which are subsidiaries of secular corporations, for whom profit, not worship value, is the most important consideration.[24]

7. *Pragmatism:* At best, CWM seems to be justified as part of a program of church growth. Advocates of CWM point to the growth of churches that use this style of music, rather than to biblical principle, to justify its use.

8. *Temporal Chauvinism:* Advocates of CWM, as those of CW, have sometimes spoken rather harshly of the historic traditions of the church. They have too eagerly set aside time-tested traditions as if wisdom began with their generation, say the critics of CWM. Therefore they have abandoned the great hymns of past generations in favor of ephemeral pop-style music, as if the highest virtue were in being up-to-date.

The Concerns of the Critics

Reducing the criticisms of CWM to a brief list is helpful for the reader's comprehension, but it is somewhat unfair to the critics themselves. Such a list doesn't indicate much of the burden or spirit of their criticism. So allow me here for a while to try to enter into the heart of their motivation, as I understand it.

The critics, for the most part, are dedicated servants of Jesus Christ who treasure the gospel of Scripture. They stand in awe and reverence before their Creator; they rejoice in what God has done through Jesus, to save his people from their sins; and they thank God for his providential care over the church through its history. They sense a fellowship with the saints of past ages, particularly as they worship according to traditions tested through many centuries. Many of them are struggling against huge cultural barriers to speak the biblical message credibly to people today.

When they look at the contemporary evangelical church, they see it as weak in many ways. Constantly tempted by the me-centeredness of contemporary culture and the anti-intellectualism that evangelicalism still struggles to overcome, and confused as it is about the very nature of its own gospel, evangelicalism certainly does not seem to be in a position to overhaul the ancient worship. Ignorance of biblical teachings among contemporary Christians (particularly as opposed to past generations) is appalling. The contemporary church, dominated in many ways by its least mature members, seems capable only of capitulation to what is worst in modern culture, to turn worship of almighty God into secular entertainment or into something hardly distinguishable from it.

As for CWM, its subjective, personal emphasis seems a symptom of the cultural diseases of subjectivism, psychologism, and humanism. Its simplicity seems to reinforce the anti-intellectualism that continues to beset the church and the culture. The reception of CWM by the larger culture seems a symptom of professionalism and consumerism. The power of CWM to communicate to contemporary people elicits the criticism that churches use it for "pragmatic" motives. And its newness brings the charge of temporal chauvinism. Every virtue of CWM provokes a corresponding criticism.

So to many dedicated Christians today, CW and CWM are cause for heartbreak. In adopting these innovations, the evangelical church seems to be selling its heritage for a mess of pottage.

I still intend to defend CWM. But I hope that my defense will be one that hears the cries of those who sense best the rigors of the spiritual warfare in our time, who are not ignorant of Satan's devices, who are least inclined to compromise the lordship of Christ, and who seek through great exertions and tears to bring the evangelical church to maturity in Christ. Among those Christian warriors are many critics of CWM.

Certainly, however, the motivations of the critics are not perfect, any more than the motivations of those who advocate CWM. We all continue to suffer the effects of Adam's fall, and we have no goodness in ourselves. No doubt many advocates of CW and CWM are to some extent ignorant of, or even seeking compromise with, the wickedness of contemporary culture. But I don't think I am entirely mistaken when I claim to see among some CWM critics a certain amount of aesthetic snobbery, idolatry of the intellect, romanticizing of past history, denominational and theological chauvinism, and indifference to biblical principle (particularly the mandate of evangelism and the principle of intelligible communication in worship).

Both sides, then, need to learn from one another, to gain a better grasp of the application of Scripture to the difficult situations of the present day. The dialogue will demand more, not less, intellectual effort. It will require us to make some distinctions that we have overlooked in the past. And it will require a greater determination to live and worship according to biblical principle, rather than by either the human traditions of the past or the innovations of the present. Biblical principle, I believe, sometimes leads us in paths that are considered "conservative" by contemporary society, and sometimes in paths that appear "liberal" or even "radical." Our chief concern should not be to measure up to any such labels, but to hear and obey what God says to us. In these ways, I think we can learn much from the call of the CWM critics to worship according to biblical principle. But when we seek to follow biblical principle, we should be open, on the basis of Scripture, to considering alternatives different from those the church has embraced in the past.

Notes

1. My defense of CWM in this volume will be directed toward Christians in the evangelical Protestant tradition. Some of my arguments will apply to others, but to make those applications explicit would take me too far afield.

2. Alister McGrath, *Evangelicalism and the Future of Christianity* (Downers Grove, Ill.: InterVarsity Press, 1995), 19.

3. Ibid., 20.

4. For more analysis of these developments, see appendix 2.

5. This argument has been made by a good many recent writers. See Os Guinness, *Dining with the Devil* (Grand Rapids: Baker, 1993); Guinness and John Seel, *No God But God: Breaking with the Idols of Our Age* (Chicago: Moody Press, 1992); Michael Horton, *Made in America* (Grand Rapids: Baker, 1991); Horton, ed., *Power Religion: The Selling Out of the Evangelical Church?* (Chicago: Moody Press, 1992); Horton, *In the Face of God* (Dallas: Word, 1996); John MacArthur, *Ashamed of the Gospel* (Wheaton, Ill.: Crossway, 1993); Ken Myers, *All God's Children and Blue Suede Shoes* (Wheaton, Ill.: Crossway, 1989); Frank Schaeffer, *Addicted to Mediocrity* (Westchester, Ill.: Cornerstone Books, 1981); Doug Webster, *Selling Jesus: What's Wrong with Marketing the Church* (Downers Grove, Ill.: InterVarsity Press, 1992). The most elaborate and influential formulation has been in the two books of David Wells, *No Place for Truth* (Grand Rapids: Eerdmans, 1993) and *God in the Wasteland* (Grand Rapids: Eerdmans, 1994).

6. Wells, *No Place for Truth,* 118, 142, 172, 174, 264, 268, 278, 280, and many other places; *God in the Wasteland,* 101–11.

7. *God in the Wasteland,* 88–117.

8. Marva Dawn, in *Reaching Out Without Dumbing Down* (Grand Rapids: Eerdmans, 1995), refers often to Wells and others to underscore what she considers to be the anti-intellectualism of many contemporary churches. See also

Mark Noll, *The Scandal of the Evangelical Mind* (Grand Rapids: Eerdmans, 1994).

    9. *God in the Wasteland,* 61, 77–84, 115, 153, 176, 202.

    10. Ibid., 60–87. Wells refers to the Church Growth Movement, particularly the writings of George Barna, as chief suppliers of marketing information for would-be contemporary churches.

    11. Ibid., 63–87, 100.

    12. Ibid., 67.

    13. *No Place for Truth,* 53–92, and Wells's other accounts of "modernity."

    14. Ibid, 11.

    15. Ibid., 218–57.

    16. *God in the Wasteland,* 88–117.

    17. *No Place for Truth,* 95–136; *God in the Wasteland,* 186–213.

    18. *No Place for Truth,* 250–57; *God in the Wasteland,* 149–51.

    19. *No Place for Truth,* 113–15.

    20. As with CWM, I am using this phrase as a technical term, not to be taken literally. It denotes, not every form of worship carried on in the contemporary world, but a certain type of worship that seeks specifically to engage the interest of people in some subcultures (mostly white and suburban) of contemporary America.

    21. Marva Dawn, to her dismay, counts twenty-eight occurrences of "I" in one song. See my discussion in appendix 1.

    22. Horton, *In the Face of God,* 124.

    23. Some have even worried that CWM songs praise the worshipers rather than God. See appendix 1.

    24. Contemporary Christian musicians and music executives have themselves complained about the secularization and commercialism of the present Christian music industry. See, for example, Michael Card and Steve Taylor, "Who's the Leader of This Band?" *Christianity Today* (May 20, 1996), 22–25, and Stan Moser, "We Have Created a Monster," *Christianity Today* (May 20, 1996), 26–27. See chap. 6 of this book.

CHAPTER 5

✤

CWM and Modern Culture

In the remainder of the book, I will be replying to the criticisms of CWM listed in chapter 4, but not necessarily in the order presented there. The first matter for our consideration will be the broad issue of whether CWM is best understood as an accommodation to what is worst in modern culture.

Likeness and Unlikeness

In one sense, it is obvious that CWM is part of modern culture. It is possible to define modern culture so broadly as to include everything under that concept, including CWM, and, indeed, including ourselves. But in narrower uses of the language we do distinguish, within contemporary society, pro-cultural from counter-cultural influences. Serious Christians aspire to be counter-cultural in that they reject the secularism that dominates our time and seek to replace it with biblical faith and life.

To be effective, however, as a counter-cultural force, it is necessary to be *like* the culture in significant ways. For one thing, it is simply not possible for someone to live in a culture without being in some ways like that culture. And there has never been a form of church music that has been unrelated to the influences of its culture. But more significantly, Scripture itself indicates that the apostles sought to be like others in their culture in certain respects. They preached God's Word in the common languages of their day,[1] and the apostle Paul sought to "become all things to all men, so that by all possible means I might save some" (1 Cor. 9:22).

Both Paul and the Corinthians were "like" the prevailing culture, in various ways. But Paul criticizes many of the accommodations of the Corinthians while justifying his own. The Corinthians sought the "wisdom of the world" (1:20); they wanted to be "wise by the standards of this age" (3:18). They sought riches and status and looked down on Paul, who accepted suffering for Christ's sake (chap. 4). They tolerated sexual immorality "of a kind that does not occur even among pagans" (5:1), and so on. The issue between the Corinthians and Paul was not *how much* they should or shouldn't be similar to the world, but *in what way* they should and should not be similar. The issue is normative, not quantitative.

So it will not settle anything to make the obvious observation that CWM is "like" some modern pop music.[2] We must assess that likeness according to the standards of God's Word. Is it a righteous likeness, such as Paul's attempt to be all things to all men? Or is it a wicked likeness, such as the Corinthians' attempt to emulate the wisdom of the world?

Culture Is Not Neutral

In discussions of these matters, friends have often reminded me that culture is never neutral. Aspects of worship like the architecture of the worship building, clothing, posture, formal or informal atmosphere, or music style can have the effect of bringing the world's values into the church, or of making a counter-cultural statement. Sometimes, churches will unthinkingly include things in worship that, seen in the context of the surrounding culture, strike precisely the wrong note. I agree with this point in general. Certainly worship should be ordered thoughtfully, and with an awareness of what conveys or confronts the values of the surrounding culture.[3]

From this important consideration, however, we should not infer that there is only one way to conduct worship without cultural compromise. It is not evident to me that there is only one style of church architecture, or one order of worship, or one standard for the clothing of worshipers, or one music style, that alone conveys the distinctiveness of the gospel in the contemporary world. Certainly we should not assume that there is compromise whenever we notice any degree of likeness to our cultural environment.

So let us ask, in terms of biblical criteria, whether the likeness of CWM to some recent[4] popular music is a good or bad thing. Some have argued that anything coming out of modern "popular" culture (as opposed to high art or folk culture) is somehow debased and unworthy of Christian worship. But that argument seems to me to spread the critical net far too wide. For one thing, as we saw in chapter 1, CWM is influenced by folk traditions as well as pop music. For another, I simply cannot detect in the better CWM songs (some of which I mentioned in chap. 3) anything (either of form or content) that recommends the anti-Christian values of contemporary culture. I don't know how to argue the point except to urge readers to listen for themselves.

Part of the problem, one that we will be noticing throughout this book, is that critics tend to argue their point in general, rather than in the specifics. One can perhaps make a historical case against pop culture in general.[5] But does that entail that congregations are somehow harmed by singing "All Hail, King Jesus," "Be Exalted, O God," "Great Is the Lord," "Great and Marvelous Are Your Works," "Though the Fig Tree Shall Not Blossom," and the rest?

Whatever these songs are, they are not mere particulars of the species "pop music." One cannot understand them without recognizing the deeply Christian spirit that has in these cases transformed the pop genre into something far better. In the original context of the 1960s Jesus Movement, these songs were profoundly *counter*-cultural. They took a style of music that had been used to express nihilistic philosophy and self-indulgence and turned it into praise of the God of Scripture.

This is not to say that every popular style with Christian words is suitable for worship. Some musical groups such as Stryper have set Christian words to heavy metal music. That may be a good evangelistic tool; it remains to be seen what God's Spirit will do with it. But in my judgment, the heavy metal style, even with Christian words, at the present time still conveys to most of us the worst in the modern rock concert scene. I cannot hear this style of music, even performed by Christians, without being harassed by emotions of anger, contempt for others, justifications for drugs, violence, perverted sex, and other forms of rebellion against God. Musically, it draws attention to the artists, as audiences marvel at the increasing outrageousness of each performance. This atmosphere may be acceptable as entertainment, but it is not easily reconcilable with the purposes of worship.

In time that may change. One day there may be forms of music historically related to heavy metal but so deeply saturated with the spirit of the gospel that they convey, by content and form, the love and justice of Jesus rather than the world's hatred of him. Perhaps in that day we will celebrate the fact that God has used these songs to bring salvation and revival. Perhaps there are beginnings of that development taking place today. I do not, however, believe that the time has come for such celebration. But I do believe that the time has come for the church to appreciate what God has done through CWM.

I can understand individual exceptions to this rule. Some Christians might have been involved in the rock scene of the 1960s and 1970s in such a way that the CWM songs actually constitute a kind of snare. Similarly, when someone is converted to Christ out of a background in classical music, Satan may use Bach chorales in worship as a means to tempt the person to idolatry. Or a former Roman Catholic monk may find in chanted psalms his individual spiritual challenge. But I do not see that CWM songs create this sort of problem in any unique degree. When one listens to the God-centered content of these songs, the counter-cultural thrust of them is obvious.

Entertainment

Sometimes when people talk of CWM bringing the world's values into the church, they are speaking of the standards of consumerism, pragmatism, commercialism, etc., which I will discuss later in this book. In a sense, the rest of this volume will be an expansion of the present chapter, because all of it will deal with aspects of the question whether CWM is too much a reflection of the worst in today's culture.

But I would like at this point to treat a fairly obvious question that comes up when we consider the value of any popular-style music in worship: Isn't this entertainment, rather than worship?

It can be, certainly, as I mentioned earlier; and we should be cautioned in this area. Entertainment is ubiquitous in our present-day culture.[6] We are used to sitting in chairs, watching and hearing people do and say clever, witty, pleasant, incredible, fun, interesting things. When we go into a church building, sit down facing forward, listen and watch, the situation is so much like that of entertainment that we are tempted to equate the two, thus bringing into worship the attitudes we bring into entertainment. So we focus on the talents of the leaders, their cleverness, skill, literary polish, pleasant personalities—anything but the presence of the Lord himself.

I have noticed that in some contemporary worship services, the praise band and lead singers will sing some songs for, say, ten or fifteen minutes, during which the congregation basically sits and listens. In one such worship period that I attended, no words to the songs were available, the leaders did not encourage us to sing, and, as I looked around me, almost nobody was singing. That type of worship seems to me to come very close to entertainment. Of course, the singers did provide material for meditation, and that was good.

Now certainly contemporary worship does sometimes draw undue attention to the wit, virtuosity, or personalities of the worship leaders and accompanists, and to the sheer musical value of the songs. Of course, this is not only a danger for contemporary worship. Traditional churches, too, have often excelled in aesthetics, and have even recommended their worship on aesthetic grounds, offering high quality music played by skilled artists, together with exciting sights and sounds of various kinds. To be honest, we would have to evaluate much of this as entertainment.

I could conclude this chapter simply by saying, "Don't do that." But the relation of entertainment to worship is not that simple. There are some criteria for good entertainment that are also criteria for God-honoring worship. In worship, sermons should be well-organized and clear, maintaining the attention of the worshipers. Music ought to be of high quality, led by skillful (1 Chron. 15:22; 2 Chron. 34:12; Ps. 33:3) artists. It should be memorable, bringing its text to dwell in the heart and mind. Those in attendance should feel welcome, among friends. Humor is sometimes valuable in worship, since there is humor in Scripture itself.[7] When these criteria are observed, worship inevitably becomes something *like* entertainment.

But as we have seen before, likeness as such is never adequate ground for criticism. And it is certainly possible to have worship services, even services with the above characteristics, that are distinguishable from entertainment per se. In such services, the vertical and horizontal purposes of worship will constantly be in the forefront. The people will be directed to expect, not *mere* amusement or admirable leaders, but the blessing of fellowship with the living God. If that happens in a service, the result will be something much greater than entertainment, and it won't much matter that some entertaining things have happened in the course of the service.

As we have seen, the problem exists for all worship styles. Bach chorales, even Gregorian chants,[8] have entertainment value. Our concern should not be to eliminate that, but to bring it into the context of a higher purpose so that worshipers virtually forget that they are being entertained.

Does CWM make it especially hard to achieve this goal? Perhaps, for those members of the congregation who regard this music style—or the Christian songs themselves—as their preferred entertainment music. In the same way, antiquarians who love Gregorian chants and attend churches that use such music need to ask God to guard their hearts, lest they get so absorbed in the aesthetic qualities of the music that they lose grip on the higher purpose of the worship. But I don't think this should be a reason to exclude chants, or Bach chorales, or Geneva Psalms, or CWM from worship. The church cannot micro-manage each individual's peculiar areas of temptation. And it is certainly possible for worship in any of these styles to point worshipers to Jesus. The words of the songs themselves do that. Certainly the CWM songs, saturated as they are with praise, press us in the right direction.

Although the confusion between worship and entertainment is a serious issue, I don't believe that the answer is an obsessive crusade to eliminate from worship anything that might be enjoyable. Some things should be eliminated, to be sure. But the result of any such obsessive crusade would be worship that is dull, uncommunicative, and inept. The sheer ugliness of this worship would be just as distracting to worshipers as an approach that sought to be as entertaining as possible. The way out of this dilemma is not negative, but positive; not eliminating all potential entertainment, but adding elements that reinforce the biblical goal of the worship.

Calvin's statement, quoted by Hart,[9] that the more a practice "delights human nature, the more it is to be suspected by believers" is to my mind too extreme, though I have some sympathy for it. "Delighting human nature" has both positive and negative possibilities, as does its contrary, "disgusting human nature." I see no reason *systematically* to favor one or the other. Our evaluation should take account of the *kinds* of delight and repulsion in a practice.

Certainly some kinds of delight are not only permissible in worship, but divinely mandated. As John Piper has reminded us,[10] God *wants* us to take delight in him (see Pss. 37:4; 40:8; 119:16, 24, 47). If our congregation does not *enjoy* hearing and singing of God's incomparable love to us in Jesus, surely something important is missing.

Notes
1. The Koine Greek of the apostles, called "fish-market Greek" by Jay Adams, was a popular language, not the language of elegant literature. But it was God's choice, well suited for communicating to all sorts of people.

2. Of course, in a philosophical sense, everything is "like" everything else in one way or other. Everything is a "being," for example. It is the degree and kind of likeness that are important.

3. For some good warnings along these lines, see Ken Myers, *All God's Children and Blue Suede Shoes* (Wheaton, Ill.: Crossway, 1989). I think, however, that at points Myers presses his case further than his logic will bear.

4. Time goes on, and one of my correspondents informs me that the soft rock of the seventies is no longer "contemporary." Radio stations classify it as "adult easy listening."

5. For my general methodological critique of the attempt to rest theological conclusions on historical analysis, see appendix 2.

6. See, for example, Neil Postman, *Amusing Ourselves to Death: Public Discourse in the Age of Show Business* (New York: Penguin Books, 1985), who shows some of the dangerous consequences of the entertainment-saturation of our culture.

7. See my *Worship in Spirit and Truth* (Phillipsburg, N.J.: P&R Publishing, 1996), 82–84.

8. Witness the remarkable recent popularity of "chant" CDs.

9. In D. G. Hart, "Reforming Worship," *Touchstone* 8:4 (fall 1995), 18.

10. In *Desiring God* (Portland, Ore.: Multnomah Press, 1986).

CHAPTER 6

❧

CWM and the Bottom Line

In this chapter I will continue the discussion of whether CWM is merely a reflection of the worst in contemporary culture. Here I am particularly interested in the charge that CWM is a symptom of consumer sovereignty, the principle that we should give people what they want in order to get large numbers of people into the church. In chapter 4 I discussed Wells's critique of "pragmatism" and the "marketing mentality" of the modern evangelical church. I believe that there is some truth at least in Wells's critique, and so it is important to ask whether, or to what extent, the spiritual ministry of CWM is compromised by these values.

CWM, the Business

There is no doubt that CWM, as part of the larger movement CCM (Christian Contemporary Music), is a major business enterprise. Jim Long, a columnist for *CCM* magazine, writes,

> Today the lines between ministry and business have become blurred. This ministry-business has become so suc-

cessful that it has attracted the attention, the dollars, and the ownership of its mainstream counterpart. Christian music is now virtually owned by the secular entertainment industry.[1]

As interviewer, Long asks a response from Michael Card, a well-known Christian artist, who comments,

> The contemporary Christian music scene used to be a song-driven industry. People would come to concerts and they would say, "Why, I heard all those songs, but I didn't know it was you who sang them." Songs tended to have a longer life in those days, and these songs were more in the possession of the church. We sang Keith Green songs and John Talbot songs in church, for example.
>
> Now, the industry is celebrity-driven. The song is almost irrelevant. The focus is on the person, and songs have become disposable. They're on the charts and play on the radio for maybe two or three weeks, but then they disappear. And now, for the most part, these songs never become a part of the church's worship. In fact, a whole other industry has grown up, like the "Praise and Worship" tapes from Integrity Music, because a need is there. And so in many ways, contemporary Christian music is becoming irrelevant. If it's irrelevant to the church, it's irrelevant as far as I'm concerned.
>
> When I look at Christian music as an industry, I'm always discouraged by it. The direction and value system are getting worse faster than any of us can imagine. There's no community in Christian music, but instead there's competition, commercialism, and individualism.[2]

Card adds, however:

> That's the bad news. The good news is, thankfully, there are still many people in Christian music who love the Lord and are driven by a call.[3]

Card here describes the gradual distinction over the last ten years between CWM and CCM: CCM, the highly commercial vehicle for artists appearing in concert and making records; CWM, the movement developing contemporary songs for Christian worship. CCM is celebrity-driven, CWM song-driven. But of course CWM is commercial too. It too is recorded and published by divisions of large, secular corporations. There is considerable overlap between CCM and CWM in composers, artists, publishing, recording. So if CCM has been subject to a decline in values, as Card says, it is certainly possible that CWM has been affected similarly.

Card's comments about these movements' relation to the church are also worth noting. Unlike CCM in general, CWM songs are used in churches. But CWM, like CCM, has developed apart from the oversight of the church, so the question arises whether its goals are the goals of the corporations rather than of the church.

All of this is cause for concern, certainly, and prayer. Is it, however, reason for us to exclude CWM from worship? I think not.

The fact is that Protestant hymn writing has always been the product of independent songwriters rather than a ministry of the church itself. None of the well-known hymn writers were actually called by a church to a ministry of hymn writing. And the publishing and distribution of hymns has always been a commercial enterprise. Even denominational hymnals are produced by commercial printers. We should certainly not assume that the making of profit automatically taints the integrity of composers and hymnwriters, any more than we would think that salaries compromise the ministries of pastors. As the apostle Paul tells us, "The worker deserves his wages" (1 Tim. 5:18).

Even though hymn writing has always come from individual initiative, the churches have certainly exercised oversight. Anybody can write a hymn, but the church has the right to decide if that hymn is to be used in worship. This is the way church oversight has operated in the past, and it continues to work in the era of CWM. Churches have the responsibility of separating wheat from chaff. They may not always take this responsibility seriously, but that is their fault, not the fault of any particular style of music.

Has the commercialization of CWM led to a decline in its quality? I cannot say that I have noticed any. Good and bad CWM songs have been written since the 1960s, and they are still being written and published today. Others may have a different opinion. I will discuss the question of quality in chapter 10. Responsible opinions, however, must be formed by examining the songs individually, not by assuming that the CWM movement is infected by larger cultural trends.[4] A good worship song does not become bad merely by its association with a commercial venture.

CWM and the Business of the Church

Another line of criticism is to the effect that the evangelical churches themselves have become too much like businesses, and that CWM is part of that development. As we have seen, Wells believes that the churches have lost sight of the theological basis of their ministry. Rather, they have followed the vision of marketers and church growth experts of attracting more people at any price. And their strategy has been to give the unchurched visitor whatever makes him or her comfortable, to be "seeker-friendly" or "user-friendly," even if that leads to compromise in the message itself. Since seekers today prefer CWM to traditional hymnody, the churches adopt CWM.

Evangelicalism has had its problems in the past with people who have promised church growth through human techniques. Charles G. Finney (1792–1875) introduced "new measures" into evangelism that he believed were essential for winning souls: the "anxious bench," highly emotional preaching, praying for people by name, and so on. Traditional Presbyterians found no biblical warrant for these practices and thought that Finney's methods compromised the sovereignty of God in bringing conversion.

I am not an advocate of Finney's methods or his idiosyncratic, semi-Pelagian theology. But I am concerned that the debate over Finney has led to some confusion among Calvinistic evangelicals. Granted that human techniques don't save anybody, apart from God's grace. Does that imply that techniques play no role in God's economy? To say that is to draw a wedge between divine sovereignty and human responsibility. As I indicated in chapter 2, God does make use of human techniques, in preaching and other forms of ministry, as means of grace to lead people to Jesus and to help them grow as Christians.

So there should be no a priori objection to the use of techniques to better communicate the Christian message. What about "seeker-friendliness"? D. G. Hart comments that "this commitment to making the gospel accessible deforms and trivializes Christianity, making it no better than any other commodity exchanged on the market."[5] Another critic, Mark Beach, after telling his readers about a "semi-erotic" song offered at a contemporary service, comments,

> No doubt, not all advocates for "contemporary worship" have any intention of sinking to such levels. But what may we expect when people, even well intentioned ones, attempt to turn the God of the Bible into a *User-Friendly God?* In just this way, the church robs both churched and unchurched people alike of the Living Lord of life.[6]

I shall discuss the orthodoxy of CWM at greater length in the following chapter. Here I only wish to show that the attempt to "make the gospel accessible" does not, in itself, violate the norms of Scripture. Therefore this attempt does not necessarily transform Christianity into a different religion.

I argued in chapter 2 that there are ways and degrees in which the Bible actually warrants seeker-friendliness,[7] for it teaches us to become like a Jew to the Jews and like a Greek to the Greeks. This doesn't mean that we are to satisfy all the wants of the unchurched. Very few planners of contemporary worship, certainly, try to go that far. If they did, they would have to eliminate from the service everything that is distinctively Christian. But it is not a bad thing to satisfy *some* of the wants of visitors, when in doing so we compromise no biblical principle and gain a greater opportunity to communicate an authentic Christian message.[8]

Obviously more needs to be said about what kinds of user-friendliness do and do not compromise the truth of the gospel. But the critics are not very helpful in this task. Seen as a critique of the whole contemporary worship movement, their comments are absurdly harsh. Seen as a critique of *part* of that movement, those comments may have a point. But then the critique is not of contemporary worship as such, but of some forms of it. And how do we distinguish the good from the bad? The critics give us no help.

If they are campaigning against the "health and wealth" preachers, or promoters of the "gospel of self-esteem,"[9] they will get no argument from me. Those movements are heretical down to their bones. They do indeed preach "another gospel" and deserve the Pauline anathema. But surely these movements are on the fringe of contemporary religion. Although they may use contemporary styles of worship and CWM, they are not really a part of evangelicalism. Surely it is not right to blame the contemporary worship movement as a whole because some of their practices are imitated by non-Christian cults.

So it seems that the criticisms in question are based either on (1) exaggerations of the "user-friendly" idea and of its detrimental effects, or (2) mistaken identification of the contemporary worship movement with the health and wealth gospel. Is there anything else behind this criticism?

The Church Growth Movement

The concept of user-friendliness is often connected with the Church Growth Movement (CGM). The CGM is the focal point of much of the criticism of the "marketing mentality" in modern evangelicalism. One leader of that movement is George Barna, one of whose books is titled *User Friendly Churches: What Christians Need to Know About the Churches People Love to Go To.*[10] I do think that much of the controversy over contemporary worship and CWM arises from concerns about the CGM. The CGM has tried to make an empirical study of growing churches, seeking to define what these churches have in common. CGM writers report these studies, sometimes advertising them (as Finney advertised his techniques) as more-or-less sure paths to increased church attendance. Critics of the movement urge that it does not do justice to divine sovereignty. CGM literature, they say, often makes it sound as if churches can gain faithful members through a series of human techniques; or worse, as if God were available to be "used," to release his power at the behest of human technicians.

I will not be able here to give any kind of thorough evaluation of the CGM. Certainly I will not defend all of the statements quoted by the critics. The CGM certainly has some problems here. We need to be very clear on the fact that God builds his church as he wills, and that he is not dependent on any human technique. Indeed, speaking empirically, God often surprises us by bringing growth to churches that break all the rules. Most of us, I'm sure, can give some examples.

On the other hand, empirical studies can certainly be informative, as we seek to become "all things to all men that by all means we should save some." CGM studies show that church attendance tends to level off when it reaches 80 percent of the seating capacity of the auditorium. This does not mean, of course, that God himself is bound to this rule. We all know of churches that are bursting at the seams, yet continue to grow. But if it is scripturally legitimate to build more worship space, or to go to two services, the leadership of the church needs to make rough and ready decisions as to when these changes normally ought to be made. A church is not necessarily violating the doctrine of divine sovereignty when it chooses to make those changes in accord with the 80-percent rule.

If the CGM sometimes errs in ignoring divine sovereignty, its critics often err by neglecting human responsibility. God normally enlarges his church through human preaching and witness (Matt. 28:19–20; Rom. 10:14–17; 1 Cor. 1:21). Such human activities inevitably involve purposes and goals. In preaching, we aim to present the gospel to a certain group of people. And our goal is not merely to cover the content of the Scripture texts we expound. Our goal is to persuade and motivate others to repent and believe. Someone may object, "But repentance and faith are God's gifts. They cannot be our goals, for we have nothing to do with producing them." It is true that we do not produce faith in others. But biblical preaching is always preaching for conviction, preaching for a verdict, cogent and persuasive. So must be our preaching today as well; anything else is less than faithful to the Great Commission.

It is difficult to say how divine sovereignty makes use of human efforts in bringing salvation to people. If it is all of God, how can man play any role at all? Yet man does play a role. And if he plays any role, it must be a goal-directed, purposeful role. The opposite is random, irrational behavior. So CGM is right to tell us that we need to plan for church growth and to use those methods which have proved most effective, when they compromise no scriptural principle.

Advocates of traditional styles of church life have no trouble with such use of means in other areas. As I indicated in chapter 2, nobody would claim that preaching can be done any old way (without clarity or logical rigor, or in a language foreign to the congregation). Nobody would say that since the effect of a sermon is in God's hands, it doesn't matter how we prepare and present it. But if that is right, then there is also a legitimate use of goal-directed human behavior to accomplish the growth of churches.[11]

And so it is not wrong to select a style of worship and music intended better to communicate with worshipers in a particular community. The fact that CGM writers recommend this does not make it wrong.

At the same time, it is important for us to remember that the movement for contemporary worship and CWM is not a product of the CGM. What we now call contemporary worship arose out of revival in the 1960s. That revival led to church growth, and understandably CGM writers have noted that connection. But CWM arose independently of the CGM. It should not be criticized because of CGM's use of it and references to it.

Again, I confess unhappiness with the methods used by the critics of CWM. They draw all sorts of things together into one big conceptual lump: the health and wealth gospel, CGM's "follow-the directions" approach to church planting, goal-oriented ministry, contemporary worship, CWM. Then they present these as one large and deeply flawed religious movement that we must repudiate in toto. Therefore CWM becomes the scapegoat for everything bad in modern Christendom. In my view this kind of argument represents poor logic, theology, and ethics. It is not valid, edifying, or fair to tie everything together in this fashion. Distinctions must be made between (1) goals that do and do not compromise divine sovereignty, (2) CWM itself and the use of it by CGM writers, (3) orthodox and heretical theology in preaching and worship. When we make those proper distinctions, I doubt that we will have any basis at all on such grounds for a generalized critique of CWM.

Marketing

Does Scripture condemn all "marketing" techniques in setting forth the gospel? Well, that depends on what you mean by marketing techniques. Certainly there are similarities between selling and preaching. (To say that is, of course, to say very little: everything is similar to everything else in one respect or other!) Both activities convey information. Both seek to elicit a commitment. Both require a speaker to attract the attention of his audience. If "marketing techniques" are simply rules for clear communication, vivid ways of attracting attention and motivating commitment, then they should certainly be taught to preachers. As I have indicated, none of this violates the doctrine of the sovereignty of God.

Now of course there are also many respects in which evangelism is different from marketing. The church's "product" is very different, eternally urgent, the ultimate in divine blessing. Our approach to communication should reflect the solemnity and holiness of our God. It should reflect our own willingness to humble ourselves in order to exalt the Lord. In these respects, we leave the secular marketing world far behind.[12]

Sometimes, then, we would do well to learn from the marketers, sometimes not. When marketers tell us that it is unwise to fill an auditorium beyond 80 percent of its capacity, we do well to listen, though we must never put such advice on a par with God's Word. Scripture never says that we must fill our buildings to the point of standing room before going to two Sunday morning services or two assemblies or a larger facility. So there is nothing wrong in taking the marketers' advice in the absence of more important considerations. But if marketers tell us we must avoid the subject of sin in order to keep the seekers comfortable, we must at that point disagree in the sharpest terms, for biblical principle is then at stake.

Is it wrong for preachers to address "felt needs" as an opening to preaching the gospel? John MacArthur has written that in worship "that is no time to entertain the lost, amuse the brethren, or otherwise cater to the 'felt needs' of those in attendance."[13] Well, many felt needs today are genuine spiritual needs according to Scripture. People want to know how to make marriages work; the Bible answers that need (Eph. 5:22–33). People want to know how to avoid anxiety; Scripture addresses that concern (Phil. 4:6–7). Why should preachers not address these topics and answer them through the riches of the gospel of Jesus Christ? Of course, many other felt needs (the "need" for health, wealth, self-esteem, etc.) are either ambiguous or condemned by Scripture. Nevertheless, even these—with their scriptural evaluations—should be the subjects of preaching.

So biblical worship and evangelism should not be viewed as simple negations of every element of an unbelieving culture. Rather, there should be a discerning use of the elements of culture, governed by the values of God's Word.

So even if the CWM style of music were recommended as a marketing tool, that would not necessarily be a bad thing. But of course it is much more than that. It is a way to reach people where they are. But it is also a way for contemporary people to worship God from the heart.

Pragmatism

The term *pragmatism* came to our attention in chapter 4. In its common use the term refers to the view that the true (and the right) is what works. The CGM is often called pragmatist, because it gives us data on what has worked in the past to increase the size of churches, sometimes seeming, at least, to claim that the same techniques can be counted on to produce church growth in other settings. This claim can be paraphrased, "Do these things because they work."

Serious Christians often condemn pragmatism. They emphasize that we should base our decisions on God's Word, not on our own observations of what works or doesn't work. But I believe more distinctions need to be made. The Bible does not give us detailed instructions for everything. It tells us to preach, but it does not give us the precise words to be used in sermons. It tells us to sing, but it does not give us all the words and music. It leaves much to our discretion.

In the previous sections of this chapter, I argued that goal-directed human choice does not conflict with the sovereignty of God. Indeed, God expects us to make choices that, in our judgment, will best accomplish his will. Scripture gives us the broad principles of behavior, including the goals we are to seek.[14] But within those limits, we ought to seek the alternatives that are likely to *work best*. To say this is only to contend for *wisdom* in the biblical sense. Wisdom begins in the fear of the Lord (Ps. 111:10) and ends in prosperity and happiness (Prov. 3:1–35). It works.

I certainly oppose any pragmatism that begins in the fear of man rather than the fear of the Lord. But once we believe God's Word, we have illumination to see what works and does not work in God's world.

In that sense, I would caution Christians against blind opposition to anyone who offers a more workable solution to a problem. On ultimate matters, we should not be pragmatists. But in matters of specific application, in which God has given us freedom to choose among alternatives, we should choose what works.

If the use of CWM in worship is contrary to any biblical principle, then we may not use it. But if Scripture permits the use of this style of music, it is not wrong to think about its pragmatic value. And as we have seen, that pragmatic value is not negligible.

Notes

1. Jim Long, "Can't Buy Me Ministry," *Christianity Today* (May 20, 1996), 20.

2. Michael Card, interviewed by Jim Long, in "Who's the Leader of This Band?" *Christianity Today* (May 20, 1996), 22.

3. Ibid.

4. I hope readers are noticing some of the recurring themes of this book, such as: (1) in criticizing CWM, we should look at specifics rather than generalities. Look at the songs individually, not merely as examples of some supposed trend. (2) Descriptions of broad cultural trends are never, in themselves, sufficient to tell us what we *ought* to do in worship. See appendix 2.

5. D. G. Hart, "Post-modern Evangelical Worship," *Calvin Theological Journal* 30 (1995), 458.

6. Mark Beach, "Contemporary Worship and the User-Friendly God (1)," *The Outlook* 45:9 (October 1995), 5.

7. To my knowledge, no defender of contemporary worship advocates belief in a user-friendly *God*. I suppose God may be said to be user-friendly in the sense that he condescends to speak to us in our language, to take our form in the Incarnation, to be open to our prayers. So understood the concept would be perfectly orthodox. But the phrase is so susceptible of misunderstanding that I would hesitate to use it in a serious theological context or to recommend its use to anybody else.

8. I believe, therefore, that John MacArthur confuses these questions when he writes, "There is simply no warrant in Scripture for adapting weekly church services to the preferences of unbelievers," in "How Shall We Then Worship?" in John H. Armstrong, ed., *The Coming Evangelical Crisis* (Chicago: Moody Press, 1996), 185. When I read such statements, I need to ask *"which* preferences"?

9. By "gospel of self-esteem" I refer to the view that people should think positively about themselves apart from God's grace. Scripture teaches, on the contrary, that apart from grace there is nothing good in us. There is, however, also a legitimate kind of self-esteem. Believers in Christ should learn to recognize themselves as sons and daughters of God, clothed in Jesus' righteousness, filled with his new life.

10. Ventura, Calif.: Regal Books, 1991.

11. I am reminded of the efforts of William Carey, founder of the modern missions movement, to convince his hyper-Calvinistic superiors of the legitimacy of "using means for the conversion of the heathen." It is hard for us to imagine today how that could have been an issue. *Of course* God uses means—"faith comes by hearing the message" (Rom. 10:17). But the mistaken impulse to oppose divine sovereignty to human responsibility still appears regularly in theological and popular Christian literature.

12. Although this sort of self-abasing servant-attitude deserves to be a model for Christians even in the marketing field!

13. MacArthur, "How Shall We Then Worship?" 185. On "entertainment" and "amusement," see chap. 5 of this book.

14. This sentence sets my "pragmatism" over against philosophical pragmatisms such as those of C. S. Peirce, William James, and John Dewey.

CHAPTER 7

&

Is CWM Authentically Christian?

In the previous chapter we heard some very harsh criticisms of contemporary worship (CW), particularly that the object of CW is a "user-friendly God," as opposed to the God of the Bible. We recall that according to Mark Beach, contemporary worship "robs both churched and unchurched people alike of the Living Lord of life."[1] We noted Hart's statement that "this commitment to making the gospel accessible deforms and trivializes Christianity, making it no better than any other commodity exchanged on the market." Marva Dawn speaks of the danger of our giving people "less of a gospel"[2] or "an inferior gospel"[3] in connection with what she considers inferior worship. Dawn is mainly concerned with the broader movement of contemporary worship, rather than with CWM as such. So we should not take comments like these as straightforward criticisms of CWM. But it is clear that Dawn and others think that CWM emerges in the context of a doctrinally lax approach to worship and therefore is in danger of communicating something less than authentic Christian teaching.

Beach quotes theologian Cornelius Plantinga, a rather infre-

quent visitor to the pages of the conservative *Outlook,* on the
changes introduced into worship by the contemporary approach.

> . . . if the popular changes, at least in the more aggressive
> forms—if the changes *do* represent a contextualized ver-
> sion of the Christian faith, then we are going to have to
> face the fact that the Christian faith is a very different re-
> ligion from the one that most of us have learned. We
> learned a religion that acknowledged creation, sin and
> grace, with God's glory as the main ingredient and human
> happiness as a wonderful, but not guaranteed, by-product.[4]

Plantinga pictures a seeker leaving a "fairly heavy duty" contemporary service saying,

> *Now* I understand what the Christian faith is all about: it's
> not about lament, or repentance, or humbling oneself be-
> fore God to receive God's favor. . . . The Christian faith
> is mainly about celebration and fun and personal growth
> and five ways to boost my self-esteem.[5]

Now of course my specific subject is CWM, rather than "contemporary worship" in general. But plainly these criticisms of
contemporary worship are intended to include CWM, or "much"
of it. Taken as such, these are very serious charges: "an inferior
gospel," "robbing" the worshipers of "the Living Lord of life,"
"a very different religion" from orthodox Christianity, a religion
without "creation, sin and grace," devoid of "repentance," favoring only "fun and personal growth and . . . self-esteem." These
people are saying that contemporary worship preaches "another
gospel" (Gal. 1:6–9), which merits only condemnation, anathema.
It presents a gospel without the Lord; without creation, sin, and
grace; without repentance; catering to the self-indulgence of the
people. Is it possible that CW, including CWM, amounts to idolatry, that it is not Christian at all?

If any of this were true of contemporary worship, we should
certainly avoid it like the plague. Of course, these writers hedge

their bets somewhat. Dawn, as we have seen, speaks typically of "much" contemporary worship. Plantinga limits his critique to the "more aggressive forms" and the "fairly heavy duty" services. Beach admits that "not all" advocates of contemporary worship sink to the lowest levels; but he thinks that even (many of?) the well-intentioned ones replace the God of the Bible with a "user-friendly" God.

If there is any doubt, I want to preface my remarks by saying that I too am concerned with maintaining authentic Christian worship. Certainly we must worship the God of the Bible and him alone. Together with the writers mentioned above, I am grieved at the level of heresy that has entered the professing church. I agree with the late J. Gresham Machen that modern liberal theology, which, in various updated forms, still dominates the major denominations and influences professing evangelical churches, is not Christianity at all, but a different religion.[6] And as I said in the previous chapter, I repudiate the "health and wealth gospel" and the "gospel of positive thinking," which remove from the gospel both heaven and grace, transforming Christianity into a self-help scheme for successfully laying up treasures on earth. These have entered supposedly evangelical churches with alarming force.

Some of these heresies have made use of CW styles and CWM. Perhaps, then, the critics mentioned above have made the mistake of associating CW and CWM with these falsifications. If they have, that is certainly a mistake. The Mormons, Jehovah's Witnesses, Christian Scientists, and Protestant liberals adopted the forms of nineteenth-century Protestant worship. Certainly that doesn't prove that this worship itself is conducive to heresy or promotes it. The same is true of attempts to correlate CW with the false gods of our time. To show that, one would have to put forth research that demonstrates a close correlation between heretical theology and CW. But the critics I cite do not offer that kind of verification for their claims.

Indeed, I do not think that the main concern of these critics is to link CW with false gospels of health, wealth, and positive thinking. Their criticism is somewhat more subtle than that. Their main problem seems to be with the *emphasis* of contemporary worship. In the material quoted above, Plantinga speaks of what the Christian faith is "mainly about," what is the "main ingredient," and what is the "by-product." So we should give some consideration to the question of "emphasis."

Emphasis and Substance

Plainly, Christian worship ought to reproduce, in general,[7] the emphasis of the biblical message itself. Scripture is a book that deals with many topics, among them the dynasties of Egypt and Babylon, the climate of Palestine, the motions of the stars, the moral problems of the inhabitants of Crete. But none of these constitutes the heart of the biblical gospel, which is that God has graciously saved his people from their sins by the blood of his Son. Certainly this message should be the heart of worship also, as we gather to praise God for this wonderful gift and to pledge ourselves to thankful service.

To say that, however, leaves other questions open for discussion. For example, granted that the gospel itself is to be our chief emphasis, that gospel has many aspects and applications. There are many sins of which it convicts us, many aspects of God's nature and work by which salvation comes to us, many forms of service that it motivates. Within the main gospel emphasis, therefore, there are many possible emphases among the aspects and applications of the gospel. No worship service can focus on all of these specifics; so worship should be varied from week to week. That is to say, at the specific level, there should be many emphases, not just one. We should not expect all services to be the same or to focus on precisely the same things.[8]

Now both CW and traditional worship (TW)(I am thinking chiefly of the Reformed tradition, that of Beach and Plantinga, as well as myself) emphasize the biblical gospel, in my opinion. Certainly CWM does. In chapter 3 I documented the God-centeredness of CWM. Here I would add that a brief perusal of MMPCB reveals songs dealing with many aspects of the gospel: the person of Christ (focus of many praise songs), his incarnation, his death as a sacrificial atonement (many songs about Jesus as Lamb of God or as giving his life for us), the Resurrection, Jesus' session at God's right hand, God's creating new hearts within us (arrangements of Ps. 51, prayer that God will "Purify My Heart," etc.), the forgiveness of sins through Jesus, assurance that we are children of God through Christ, the church as the body of Christ, expressions of trust, exhortations to consecration, prayer for the coming of God's kingdom, the spiritual warfare being fought today between God's people and the Evil One.

As I mentioned in chapter 3, CWM does not excel in its breadth of doctrinal coverage; this is one reason why I believe that CWM should not replace traditional hymnody. There are some rather striking omissions in MMPCB. I was unable to find any song specifically referring to justification by faith alone, though there are many songs proclaiming the merits of Christ's life and death as the righteous Lamb and expressing our faith in him alone. Another remarkable omission in MMPCB: I cannot find any song focused upon Jesus' second coming.[9] That is surprising, because it would seem that songs about Jesus' glorious return would be right up the alley of the praise-song composers. Our congregation does, however, sing a good praise song from outside MMPCB on the theme "Come Quickly, Lord."[10] At the same time, I am usually better able to find musically adequate songs about the doctrine of adoption in MMPCB than in the traditional hymnals. I also believe that CWM provides, on the whole, better selections than traditional hymnody on the subjects of humility, servanthood, and love for other believers.

Nevertheless, it is clear that all of these topics represent aspects of the gospel of salvation from sin through Jesus Christ. I certainly see no tendency in this literature to substitute for the gospel of salvation a religion without "creation, sin and grace," devoid of "repentance," favoring only "fun and personal growth and . . . self-esteem."[11] There may be some contemporary worship services that yield this impression, but if this criticism has any validity as a broad criticism of CW, one would certainly expect this self-centered mentality to be at least slightly visible in its hymnody.

And as a criticism of CWM, I believe that this kind of language is downright slanderous.

I am willing to concede that there are differences of "emphasis" between TW and CW. This difference is certainly not the difference between an emphasis on the gospel and an emphasis on fun and personal growth and self-esteem. It is, rather, a difference of emphasis among the *aspects* of the gospel, that second level which we discussed above. The main difference in emphasis is that CW is, like the Sunday worship of the early church, primarily a celebration of the Resurrection.[12] Thus there is a large emphasis on joy, celebration. The veil of the temple is torn in two, and we may enter there boldly to fellowship with the One who recognizes us as his children and friends. The dark side of Christian experience still exists, but it is brought to the feet of the risen Jesus, who is forever victorious over sin and death. TW, on the other hand, tends to focus on our pre-Resurrection relationship with God. God is more distant, more disapproving. He is hidden, and we are unclean, unfit to enter his holy place. We are lost, without hope. As a kind of re-enactment, at least, we need to be saved from sin again by believing the gospel and finding forgiveness. Then we hear the assurance of pardon and receive the promise of reconciliation with God. Then we may experience some of the joys of the post-Resurrection experience, until next Sunday.

I would not say that the emphasis of TW is wrong, although the reader has probably gathered from my language my preference for the emphasis of CW. There is some value, certainly, in the re-enactment of the history of redemption from Creation and Fall through Resurrection and Second Coming, and there is room for different emphases among the various aspects of the gospel. Perhaps CW churches should be urged to follow the TW model on some occasions. But CW addresses us where we are, in the New Covenant, as sinners already saved by God's grace, raised with Christ to newness of life. Can anybody argue that that emphasis is harmful? Certainly no thoughtful Christian can claim that this emphasis is heterodox or lacking in Christian authenticity. To say that it "robs both churched and unchurched people alike of the Living Lord of life," "deforms and trivializes Christianity," or that it presents "less of a gospel" or "an inferior gospel" betrays at best the speaker's ignorance, false criteria, or bad temper.[13]

God in CWM: A Rock Star?

With all this talk ringing in our ears, we should remind ourselves of the discussion in chapter 3 to the effect that CWM is God-centered. CWM is pre-eminently praise music, though there are other themes as well in the genre. I think it is obvious that the God of CWM is the God of the Bible, but some critics, like the above, have questioned that. One correspondent of mine, whom I shall call Historicus, presents an interesting form of the argument that CWM honors a false god. He finds that CWM models God after the image of a rock star. I think his argument ultimately fails, but it will be worth discussing, since Historicus states well some thoughts that others might find themselves sharing.

Historicus says,

> The Praise song fantasizes a relationship of the worshiping believer to God by claiming the relationship while ignoring the entire biblical message of conditions and consequences. In this sense it "decontextualizes" praise of God by removing it from its complete biblical context. Praise songs parallel popular music's theme of a fantasized relationship of the frenzied listener to the rock star idol or performer. . . .
>
> The listener desires a relationship with the star, fantasizes it to be and emotes over such a relationship while suppressing the reality that such a relationship can never occur and will never occur. The star does not know of the desired relationship and certainly never granted it.

Historicus goes on to describe this relationship as individual, rather than corporate: the listener denies the existence of any competing lovers or "fantasizes them to be dead, defeated, discarded or annihilated." He pursues this fantasy obsessively, fleeing his responsibilities in the real world.

This fantasizing is, of course, quite contrary to Christianity, in which "the poetry and music of true worship extol the divine gift and bestowing of the love relationship and delight in telling of its conditions, its birth, its development and its fruitfulness." The Christian believer recognizes that "millions of other believers have been given a parallel love relationship and he/she delights in responsible, loving thoughts and actions toward those other members of the family of God." He or she endures sadness as well as happiness and takes responsibility to pursue a divine calling in the real world.

Praise songs, says Historicus, generally avoid the preconditions of a person's relationship to God (prevenient grace, conviction of sin, repentance, saving faith, the conversion experience, a holy fear of God), the consequences of faith in Christ (obedience, service, desire for the salvation of others, strength to bear burdens, the Spirit's indwelling), and discussion of our future (social goals, heaven and hell).

Praise songs, he says, assume that every worshiper is already saved "and thus are especially dangerous to unbelievers and even seekers who need a more nearly complete account of the Christian faith." They express praise without focus on its preconditions. They create a privatized channel to God. "Many" praise songs are so nonspecific they could be sung by Buddhists. They present, at best, "sound bites," with no reflection, development, or application. And they ignore the biblical narratives of the Gospels and Acts of the Apostles, neglecting the doctrines of the crucifixion, resurrection, ascension, and bodily return of Christ. Finally, they are egocentric, overusing words like I, me, we, us.

Historicus is certainly onto something here. He has noticed, as I have pointed out in this book, that CWM is not strong in "doctrinal coverage." These songs focus on praise, and when they speak of doctrines and events of redemptive history they tend to focus on one or two per song, rather than a great many as in traditional hymnody. Nevertheless, as we have seen, you can find hymns in the CWM literature that deal with almost any redemptive event, ethical theme, human condition, or theological doctrine.

In MMPCB, the first song (Dave Moody's "All Hail, King

Jesus") speaks of our reign with Christ throughout eternity (negating Historicus's point that CWM songs never speak of heaven). Song 2 (Graham Kendrick's "Shine, Jesus, Shine") speaks of Jesus as light of the world and bringer of truth, our entrance into his brightness by his blood, our future destiny to change from glory to glory, our desire that our lives might mirror that glory and tell God's story to others. The chorus calls for God to flood the nations with his grace, his mercy, and his Word. This song certainly does not fantasize any privatized relation to God. It speaks clearly of the preconditions of that relationship and its consequences both for today and for the future, in the "real world."

Song 4, "All Heaven Declares," by Noel and Tricia Richards, adores Christ's glory and beauty as the risen One, the Lamb upon the throne, "who once was slain to reconcile man to God." Surely here the conditions of the love relationship are clearly in view.

There are many CWM songs that speak of the church as a loving family of God in which believers take responsibility for and care for one another. The MMPCB topical index lists fifteen songs of this kind, and of course there are many in other books. In MMPCB there are many songs that speak of obedience and commitment to the Lord (fifteen in the index), including settings of 2 Chronicles 7:14, Micah 6:8, Matthew 6:33, 1 Peter 5:5–6. As I mentioned earlier, there are several settings of the Apostles' Creed and the Lord's Prayer. Psalm 51 is quoted in several songs, asking God to forgive our sins and create in us clean hearts. Many songs focus on Jesus' shedding his blood in atonement. There are plenty of songs that acknowledge God's majesty and awesome greatness.

Historicus is correct to say that for the most part CWM songs assume that the worshipers are already saved. That should surprise nobody; that is true of most traditional hymnody, as well, and is biblically proper. As I indicated in chapter 2, the worship service is primarily for believers, though some thought should be given to seekers who visit the service. It is typical of critics of CWM to see the songs as being too much directed toward seekers; Historicus sees them as being written exclusively with Christian worshipers in mind. I think that both views are extreme, in addition to being inconsistent with one another. CWM songs are songs that believers sing in praise to God *and therefore* in testimony to the world (this is sometimes called "doxological evangelism"). It can be a powerful witness to non-Christians to observe Christians fervently praising their God. CWM songs take both audiences into consideration by putting believers' songs into language understandable to the unbeliever.

I doubt if there are many, if any, praise songs that could be sung as well by Buddhists. Or does Historicus mean to say that CWM songs could easily be converted into hymns acceptable to Buddhists? Of course, one could always change "Praise the Lord" to "Praise Buddha." George Harrison in "My Sweet Lord" interchanged "Hallelujah" with "Hare Krishna." Presumably he could have done that in any hymn where the word "Hallelujah" appears, including Handel's Hallelujah Chorus. Does that mean that "Hallelujah" is unacceptable as a term of Christian praise? I don't think so.

We have seen that praise songs are often explicitly Trinitarian, that they speak of Jesus' atonement, his resurrection, the Spirit's indwelling, etc. These songs are not religiously nonspecific.

Historicus's essay reinforces my belief that most of the critics of CWM don't know CWM very well. They have bought into certain common myths about CWM, which appear plausible because of the songs' focus on praise and the limited doctrinal coverage of each song. They have also, perhaps, seen too close a relationship between CWM and Church Growth theory, and they therefore assume that CWM must be part of a conspiracy to dumb down worship and to appeal to the depraved wants of the unbeliever. But that view is easily refuted by a survey of the songs themselves.

Historicus also appears to assume that churches which use CWM use it exclusively. Many churches do, but in my own church and in many others CWM is used together with traditional hymns in a fruitful interrelation. CWM publishers themselves have been recommending this combination in recent years. I believe it is beneficial in worship to include both longer hymns that cover large doctrinal areas and shorter ones that focus on a few points with more emotional power and vividness. For the former purpose, traditional hymns are generally best in our present situation, and CWM for the latter purpose. That way, the music addresses a wide range of ages, tastes, levels of spiritual maturity, and types of spiritual need. Even though CWM covers much more doctrinal territory than Historicus imagines, he is right to point out that traditional hymnody offers more choices in some areas of biblical teaching.

However, Historicus is certainly unsuccessful in his attempt to prove that CWM inculcates a radically different religion from historic Christianity. CWM's God is the God of Scripture, not a fantasized rock star. The distinctively biblical character of CWM is evident to the most superficial observer who is willing simply to open MMPCB and flip through it.

Reverence and Joy

There are some who question the Christian authenticity of CW and CWM on the ground that these are not sufficiently filled with "reverence and awe" (Heb. 12:28). Certainly authentic worship of the biblical God must recognize his majesty and supreme dignity. Does CWM rightly represent him?

I confess that I have always found reverence to be one of the *strengths* of CWM. The emphasis on praise, on God's transcendence, his sovereignty, holiness, majesty, and power, is very strong. Of course, there is also an emphasis on God's immanence: God with us, Immanuel. He is near to us in providence. He dwelt with Israel in the tabernacle and temple. He "tabernacled" with us in the incarnation of Christ (John 1:14). His Spirit dwells in Christian believers as his temple (1 Cor. 3:16–17; 6:19; 2 Cor. 6:16; Eph. 2:21). We are still to fear him as the Holy One, worshiping in reverence and awe (Heb. 12:28–29). But in Christ the veil of the temple is torn in two (Matt. 27:51), and believers are called to enter "boldly" into the holiest place, which struck terror into the hearts of pious Israelites (Heb. 4:16). We are not only servants of Christ, we are also friends (John 15:13–15). The church's witness must honor both God's transcendence and his immanence. We must worship in awe and wonder, but also in boldness and holy joy (Ps. 2:11). Like the other balances of emphasis we have considered in this chapter, that balance is not always easy to achieve. But we must not simply emphasize one aspect to the exclusion of the other.

David Wells in his critique of contemporary evangelicalism accuses the churches of insufficiently emphasizing transcendence. But he says very little about God's immanence, or about how it is related to his transcendence in worship. Wells seems to fear that to emphasize God's immanence—his friendship with us in Christ—is to say that God can be manipulated, used, forced to fit into our programs. But actually it is to say precisely the reverse. We are to teach about God what he has authorized us to teach about him, neither adding nor subtracting anything (Deut. 4:2; 12:32; Rev. 22:18–19).

Jollification

Another concern about CW is that there is humor in its worship, which detracts from the reverence due to God. This concern seems to lie behind Plantinga's remarks about there being in CW too much of an emphasis on "fun."

I gather that one thing Beach, Hart, Plantinga, and Dawn are saying is that when the style of worship is too happy, friendly, or fun, it misleads worshipers as to the nature of the gospel. Well, maybe so. But how happy is too happy? Must we be dour, frowning all the time? Is there no place for the biblical emphasis on joy and celebration? Is it illegitimate to mention even the humor that is undoubtedly part of the biblical text itself?[14]

No doubt there is a difference between secular jollification[15] and holy joy. It is not always easy to tell the difference, and some immature leaders of contemporary worship may substitute the former for the latter. That deserves some rebuke, though I think not the anathemas that our critics have thrown down like lightning bolts from heaven. Nor do I think this error is very widespread in contemporary worship circles. Listen to any of Integrity's Hosanna! Music tapes. The worship leaders on those tapes are clearly not seeking to amuse. Rather, they intend to draw listeners into God's holy presence, reminding them of the holiness and majesty of the God before whom they bow in worship.

But if that is the point, then the critics must take on the responsibility to (1) define the difference between jocularity and joy, and (2) direct their criticism precisely against those who fail to honor that distinction. It is simply unfair for them to bring generalized, undefined accusations, suggesting that CW as such encourages heretical deformations of the Christian faith. That is just as wrong as saying that traditional liturgy encourages sour or sanctimonious attitudes.

Popular forms of Christian music have often been criticized as "too happy." But many Psalms are joyful, and the church sings them despite the sufferings of this life. Why do we sing happy songs in a sad world? My colleague Mark Futato recently preached a sermon with that question as its title. He answered it with excellent biblical insight: We sing happy songs, not out of denial of suffering and wickedness, but out of gratitude for God's blessings in the past, and out of faith, expecting the fulfillment of God's promises in the future. We know that "our present sufferings are not worth comparing with the glory that will be revealed in us" (Rom. 8:18). The happy songs of CWM help us to express this gratitude and hope.

Is CWM Orthodox?

So far I have spoken in general terms of the doctrine of God in CWM. But we must examine Christian authenticity also in more specific doctrinal terms. Is CWM particularly prone to doctrinal error?

I could easily be persuaded that some CWM songs express false doctrine. That is true of hymns of all eras and styles. The trouble is that the critics of CWM very rarely cite specific examples of their concerns. Rather, they assimilate the entire CWM literature to their general view of CW, which supposedly trivializes God to make him user-friendly. I have questioned above that view of CW. If it is true, it seems to me odd in the extreme that such a self-indulgent movement has chosen for its musical expression a type of music that consistently repudiates self-indulgence and exalts God. Rather, in my view, the God-centeredness of CWM suggests that the critics are wrong. The broader contemporary worship movement is also essentially (with some exceptions, of course) God-centered. And since CWM is not only God-centered, but also very close to the biblical texts, as we saw in chapter 3, it is unlikely to be a fount of theological error.

Marva Dawn offers only one example of a CWM song that she thinks is doctrinally unorthodox. For her discussion and my response, see appendix 1.

We should see that despite the rather broad statements often made about the doctrinal inadequacies of CWM, it is not easy to find an actual example of heresy. Indeed, CWM is pretty successful at insulating itself from false teaching, simply by sticking close to the scriptural text. My own view is that for this reason there is probably less heresy in CWM than there is in any other tradition of hymnody.

Notes

1. Mark Beach, "Contemporary Worship and the User-Friendly God (1)," *The Outlook* 45:9 (October 1995), 5.

2. Marva Dawn, *Reaching Out Without Dumbing Down* (Grand Rapids: Eerdmans, 1995), 150.

3. Ibid., 151.

4. Beach, "Contemporary Worship," 4–5. Beach quotes Plantinga's pamphlet, *Fashions in Folly: Sin and Character in the 90s,* without providing publication data.

5. Beach, "Contemporary Worship," 5. Note that Plantinga suggests that we must humble ourselves before God "to receive God's favor"—probably a theological slip on his part, but this formulation implies works righteousness.

6. J. Gresham Machen, *Christianity and Liberalism* (New York: Macmillan, 1923; Grand Rapids: Eerdmans, 1946).

7. Of course one can never reproduce the emphasis of Scripture precisely and exhaustively except by sticking entirely to the words of Scripture and reading it from Genesis to Revelation.

8. For more on the subject of "emphasis" as a criterion for theological soundness, see my *Doctrine of the Knowledge of God* (Phillipsburg, N.J.: Presbyterian and Reformed, 1987), 182–83, 370.

9. There are certainly many songs that allude to Jesus' return as they pray for the coming of God's kingdom. Note also Steven L. Fry's "Lift Up Your Heads to the Coming King," MMPCB, 153.

10. Another song for which I have no publication information. Sorry!

11. I don't know of a single song in MMPCB about fun or self-esteem. Personal growth, yes, but only in a context of humbly trusting Jesus to lead into greater purity and devotion.

12. On this point, compare my account in *Worship in Spirit and Truth* (Phillipsburg, N.J.: P&R Publishing, 1996), 68–69.

13. There is also a difference in emphasis between CW and TW in the relative attention given in worship to evangelism and to nurture. Here too, I think that the greater emphasis of CW upon evangelism is an improvement over TW, though it may sometimes go too far. See my discussion of the Great Commission in chap. 2.

14. See *Worship in Spirit and Truth*, 82–84.

15. I'll never forget my esteemed teacher in theology, the late Professor John Murray, presenting in a devotional talk his distinction between "jollification" and "joy." He delivered the message, as he always preached, with a very dour expression, in utmost seriousness. I confess I was inwardly amused that this great saint and brilliant theologian, who had taught us so profoundly about the Reformed doctrines of justification, sanctification, and glorification, was now teaching us, with equal solemnity, the Reformed doctrine of "jollification." As one of my colleagues suggested, he was adding to the traditional systematics a *locus de ialificatio.*

CHAPTER 8

&

Does CWM Edify?

In chapter 2 I emphasized that there are in worship both vertical and horizontal foci. Worship is vertical in that its main purpose is to honor God. But it is also horizontal in that it should seek to edify the worshipers (1 Cor. 14:26). In the previous chapter we focused on the vertical perspective, asking if CWM is faithful to its Lord, honoring his transcendent majesty, reverent, true to God's revelation of himself. In this chapter and the next, I will examine the horizontal perspective to determine if CWM helps people to know the Lord and to grow in their relationship to him.

The Subjective and Objective in Worship

As we saw in chapter 4, David Wells believes that there is too much subjectivity, not enough objectivity, in the message of modern evangelicalism. This is also a frequent theme in the writings of Michael Horton, who says,

> . . . one cannot help but notice the contrast between the objective focus of orthodox Christianity and the subjective emphasis of Gnostic mysticism and romanticism. . . .

Biblical Christianity is concerned with what happened outside us, two thousand years ago, outside the city of Jerusalem. It is an "over there" religion, not an "in here" religion. It is centered on what happened externally, not on what happens internally. . . . Anything that has to do with me and my works or my experience securing victory and intimacy with God is sure to lead to despair. It is bad news, not good. And, by the way, this is not to in any way detract from the importance of the new birth or the subjective dimension of Christian experience. It is simply to say that nothing that happens within me is the gospel.[1]

I am glad that Horton qualified his argument in the next-to-last sentence. To that I reply that he could have fooled me! As for the last sentence, it seems to me to rely on an unnecessarily narrow definition of "gospel." The gospel is the good news of Jesus Christ. It is a message about what happened objectively in redemptive history. It is also the message that because of that objective salvation, we today can be transformed from within by God's Spirit.

Should the church's preaching and song focus on the objective rather than the subjective, on God and history rather than our response, on objective truth rather than human experience, as these writers argue? I have some sympathy for these arguments, for I do believe that in general evangelical preaching today needs to place a greater emphasis on the objective.

But these writers miss nuances. In theory of knowledge it is wrong to force a choice between object (what one knows) and subject (the knower). All knowledge involves both: you don't have knowledge unless you have both a subject and an object.[2] Therefore, Scripture records the objective truth of God and redemption; but it also records the experiences by which the biblical writers came to know these objective facts. And indeed there is in Scripture much teaching about the believer's subjectivity. The Psalms are full of "I" and "we," full of personal testimonies about how God has entered human experience. We learn much in Scripture about our emotional life: about joy, fear, anxiety, peace, anger, erotic passion, and so on.

In appendix 1, I discuss the relation between praising God on the one hand and declaring one's intention to praise God on the other, a distinction that I believe is misused in Marva Dawn's critique of some CWM songs. The former might be described as "objective," the latter as "subjective." But as I argue there, the differences are not that great. In praising, one reveals the intention to praise; and in declaring the intention, one inevitably engages in praise.

And there is a subjective side to salvation itself. The objective side is that Christ, the Son of God, lived a perfect human life, died for the sins of his people, rose from the dead, and ascended into heaven. The subjective side is that when he died for sin, we died to sin (Rom. 6:1–14) and rose with Christ to newness of life. God not only atones, he regenerates. We are new creatures (2 Cor. 5:17), partakers of Christ's abundant life (John 10:10). The gospel is not only about what God has done *for* us; it is also about what he does *in* us and *through* us. The Great Commission envisions the transformation of sinners into disciples. We are not only forgiven; we are changed, inside and out.

For the same reason, preaching, in Scripture, does not merely present the objective truths of the history of redemption. It also responds to those truths in a personal way, giving testimony of what God has done in the life of the preacher and what he can do in the lives of the hearers. The Psalms are full of such testimony, as are the Letters of Paul. And biblical preaching calls for its hearers to respond to it, both inwardly and outwardly. Biblical repentance is a change of heart that brings change in behavior, and it is a crucial goal of preaching (Acts 2:38–39).

The same must be said about worship music. As the Psalms indicate, it is not only legitimate, but important, to place our inner lives before God in our songs, to expose before him our emotions—of love, joy, and contentment, but also of anxiety, hatred, anger, fear, bewilderment.

Therefore, worship music is not merely a recital of things that happened objectively in history, though it is partly that. It is also a deeply subjective interaction with the God who sees our hearts.

But of course subjective responses to God's grace are not neutral: there are right and wrong ways to respond. And those who lead worship are responsible to encourage right responses. We are reminded of Wells's arguments that many churches have substituted secular psychotherapy (sometimes "baptized" psychotherapy) for the Word of God, as the solution to all human problems. Dealing with people's inner attitudes is a large responsibility, for worship leaders and preachers as well as counselors and therapists. Much damage can be done through psychological manipulation, or when people's excitements are aroused through mere emotional attraction rather than through the biblical message itself. Horton and Wells are right insofar as they seek to caution us against that.

So we need to ask whether CWM encourages godly responses to God's grace.

Does CWM Nurture Christian Character?

One way in which worship nurtures character is simply by presenting the authentic Christian message, as I emphasized in the previous chapter. But the style of worship is important too, in that it can either reinforce or detract from the message. Perhaps the central concern expressed in Marva Dawn's *Reaching Out Without Dumbing Down* is that music and worship nurture mature Christian character.[3] She says much there about the importance of truth, faithfulness to biblical teaching, honoring God as the main subject of worship, the motivation of the pastor, and so on, with which I have no quarrel. But as I have argued earlier, CWM is God-centered music and it is mostly scriptural truth in scriptural language.

As she and others point out, many of those who prefer CWM are immature. It is music of the young, and the young tend to be less mature than the old. But that's the whole point of CWM. CWM is Christian music that is immediately accessible—to the young as well as the old, to the immature as well as the mature. Therefore, as I argued in chapter 5, it is an extremely valuable tool for teaching the immature, for helping the immature to become mature.

Saying that people are immature because they sing CWM songs is like saying that children are immature because they sing songs like "The Wise Man Built His House Upon the Rock" and "Jesus Loves Me." But that is absurd. Children are immature because they are children. The genre of children's Christian music is intended, bit by bit, to instruct them and raise them out of their immaturity. For the sake of that task, it is better that children sing some children's hymns, rather than adult hymns alone. The same can be said of CWM.

Another controversy regarding the nurture of Christian character is this: Dawn and others question whether too much comfort is a distraction in worship. If we are to become serious disciples of Christ, must we not be pushed out of our comfort zone? Must we not exercise our spiritual muscles, do some things that are good for us, that we would not otherwise do?

But if we are to insist on some discomfort as a means of spiritual exercise in worship, shouldn't that burden be borne more equitably than the critics prescribe? I believe that much of the pressure to hold exclusively to traditional liturgy stems precisely from a desire for comfort. The question is, whose comfort? My wish is that all parties in the church would be more willing to sacrifice their comforts in order to love one another and to further the mission of the church. I would insist that neither the traditionalists nor the advocates of contemporaneity are perfectly sanctified. My observation (and I guess I'm as much entitled to nonspecific observations as are those on the other side) is that in traditionalist circles there is too much pride, too much indifference to those outside of Christ, too much wanting to be comfortable with one's own preferred styles. That too is immaturity, and worship ought to deal with it.

Seekers

We have earlier discussed somewhat the concepts of "user-friendliness" and "seeker-sensitivity." I have argued that such passages as the Great Commission and 1 Corinthians 14:23–25 warrant some concern to communicate with non-Christian visitors in worship. What does CWM do for them? Certainly it seeks to eliminate artificial barriers of music and text that make communication with the unchurched and the immature unnecessarily difficult. Does it then exist, as some critics claim, to make unbelievers "comfortable"? In this respect (though not in all, as we have seen), I think the case for CWM stands or falls with the argument for CW (contemporary worship) as a whole. So I shall ask, is CW user-friendly in that it seeks to make unbelievers "comfortable?"

Terms like that are not conducive to a clear understanding of what is happening here. Let's try to get a better handle on it. Take a religious survey in your neighborhood. Ask unchurched people why they don't go to church. Occasionally you will meet someone who answers pointedly that Christianity is untrue and who doesn't want anything to do with the church. But more often people give trivial and stupid reasons for not attending: The service is too early or too late or too long; the parking lot is too full; dressing up on Sunday morning is a pain; the pews are uncomfortable; the nursery is inadequate; the preacher's style is boring; the people aren't friendly enough; the liturgy is too complicated; the music is old-fashioned; the church is always begging for money; and so on.

Now I have little sympathy for these excuses. If these people understood who God really is, his wrath and his love, what he demands and what he offers, they would (or should) break down doors to worship him. My fleshly instinct is to say, "All right; just go ahead and die in your sins. Then you'll know what discomfort really is!" But, of course, that is a fleshly, not a spiritual response (cf. Luke 9:54). God's Word calls us to love people, even to love our enemies. And it calls us to consider others' interests above our own, to lay down our own lives for those of others, following the steps of Jesus to the cross.

Now Scripture does not tell us that worship must be held at inconvenient hours, that everyone must wear their best clothes, that seating must be uncomfortable. Nor does it say that our style of music and preaching must be boring, old-fashioned, unintelligible. If it did say these things, we would have to tell the unchurched, "Sorry, but we must follow Scripture, not your stupid and trivial preferences." But it doesn't say those things. It gives us freedom to be flexible in these areas.

So shouldn't we, other things being equal, adjust our worship style as much as possible to nullify those trivial objections, that is, to take away the excuses? If we love people and long to see them come to Christ, I believe that we will be willing to sacrifice our own comforts for theirs, in the interest of their salvation. Jesus certainly did.

Would that amount to making worship "user-friendly" and "comfortable"? Is it "catering to the wants of the unchurched"? Is it "pragmatism"? Perhaps it is, in a sense. But we have seen that there is a biblically warranted pragmatism, and that makes all the difference. It is becoming all things to all people that we might by all means save some. It is not a compromise of the gospel, but it is rather a way of removing unnecessary offense so that the offense of the cross itself may be heard all the more vividly, all the more offensively.

Our reason for doing these things, ultimately, is not to please the visitors, but to please and imitate the Lord. Certainly the visitors will be pleased up to a point if we do our job well, but that is hardly ground for criticism. Ultimately and eventually unbelieving visitors will be repelled by the message of the service, whatever the surface comforts, unless God regenerates their hearts.

How far should we go along this route? How far did Jesus go? We should go as far as our consciences permit as they are bound to God's Word. We may not compromise the gospel or the orthodoxy of our teaching. Nor should we adopt a style of worship that neglects the spiritual nurture of the believers and focuses entirely on the visitors. As my former pastor, Dick Kaufmann, has said, we should be "seeker-sensitive," but not "seeker-driven." Within this general perspective, there is room for freedom; different churches may legitimately make different choices in view of their own history, local culture, and the nature of their surrounding communities.

Perhaps some, even "many" churches that use CWM don't have the biblical priorities outlined above. They may be using this music without a full understanding and commitment to biblical principle. But there are plenty of liturgically conservative churches that have the same problem. The fault in both cases is not with the music as such, but with those who plan the overall ministry of the church.

Notes

1. Michael Horton, *In the Face of God* (Dallas: Word Publishing, 1996), 124.

2. And, third, a norm or standard. See my *Doctrine of the Knowledge of God* (Phillipsburg, N.J.: Presbyterian and Reformed, 1987).

3. For her discussion and my response, see appendix 1.

CHAPTER 9

❧

Does CWM Dumb Down Worship?

In this chapter I shall continue my discussion of the question of whether CWM edifies worshipers. Here the focus will be on a matter that has become central in debates over CWM: the intellectual content of the songs. As I indicated in chapter 4, evangelicalism has been embarrassed by anti-intellectualism in its history, and in the present day. This problem was greatest, I believe, between the Scopes trial and the end of the Second World War. Since then, many evangelicals have tried hard to re-establish high academic and intellectual standards, but the problem is far from completely solved.

In appendix 2, I offer more analysis of this important issue. To summarize, Protestantism was originally a movement of scholars, and they carried the study of Scripture to a higher level of precision and care. Zwingli's view of worship was based, indeed, on the model of an academic lecture. No other Reformers followed him in this concept, but they all believed that the preaching of the Word was central to worship, and they saw that preaching as having a strongly intellectual aspect.

Later, evangelicalism absorbed elements of Anabaptism,

Pietism, Arminianism, charismatic theology, and dispensational-ism, which often protested against what they regarded as a hyper-intellectualism among their fellow Protestants.

My view is that intellect is important, but it is not autonomous or supreme. Only Scripture is the self-attesting, final Word of God for human faith and life. It is Scripture that sets forth the ul-timate norms for the intellect.[1] Therefore it is Scripture that tells us how "intellectual" our worship ought to be, and in what ways it should engage the intellect.

The role of intellect in theology, worship, and the Christian life, is not somehow self-evident. There are right and wrong ways to use the intellect, and it functions differently in different situations. It will not do to say that worship (or theological education, or apologetics, or the Christian life) must be as intellectual as possi-ble. We must be concerned about factors other than the intellec-tual, and how the intellect fits into the particular situation in view.

In this chapter, we shall consider the specific situation of wor-ship. What is the role of the intellect in worship, and how should that role be advanced? Should worship songs be intellectually deep? How deep? Should they contribute to the intellectual growth of the congregation? If so, what is the best way for them to do that?[2]

The Intellect and Worship

Many important questions in this area remain unresolved. What, exactly, is this intellectual "depth" we are supposed to be seeking, and how can the musical elements of worship best communicate that depth? Let me try my hand at answering those questions as I formulate some general principles on the role of intellect in worship.

Certainly, for evangelicals, the most important question in this area is What does Scripture say? It is Scripture that limits and de-fines the use of the intellect, and establishes the standards for wor-ship.

It is very wrong to condemn or recommend a form of worship based merely on some vague cultural sense of what is "deep" and what is "shallow." Certainly it is wrong also to embrace an intellectualist concept of worship because of historical evangelical embarrassments or out of the fear of being thought stupid by the opinion-makers of modern society. Nor, of course, should we embrace an anti-intellectualism as a reaction against those opinion-makers, or out of our own mental laziness. How do we steer between these extremes? We cannot if we seek to resolve the questions autonomously. But if God's Word speaks to us on the subject, then we can make progress toward truly common criteria.

Scripture does not speak directly to the question of the intellectual level of worship. Clearly, however, biblical worship does have some intellectual aspects. The teaching of God's Word is an important part of worship, and teaching or learning always involves some mental engagement. That teaching occurs not only during sermons, but also in the songs (Col. 3:16). Indeed, all things in worship are to be done for the edification of God's people (1 Cor. 14:26); therefore, argues the apostle Paul, all worship is to be intelligible, not in uninterpreted unknown tongues.

I don't believe that teaching is a *merely* intellectual process. Intellect, emotions, will, imagination, etc. are interdependent, and therefore all of them play a role in learning.[3] The worship songs in Scripture itself—the Psalms—are highly emotional, and they are filled with exhortations to action, appeals to the will. But surely there is also a large role for what we usually call the intellect.

It does not follow, however, that worship should be carried on at some abstract "highest intellectual level." It would be absurd to claim that worship should be as intellectual as possible, in some general academic sense of *intellectual*. For then only post-doctoral researchers could understand what is going on, or perhaps not even they. Evidently, then, the intellectual level of worship must be to some extent relative to the intellectual capacities, attainments, and needs of the worshipers.

That is all the more obvious when we consider the meaning of "teaching." A good teacher is not somebody who speaks a rarefied, perhaps archaic, intellectual jargon that no student can understand. Rather, an effective teacher speaks the present language of his students. He may try to teach them the technical language of a field if he deems it important to their progress in the course. But he starts where they are. He begins with what they know and then moves on to what they don't know. Dawn understands this point well.

> Indeed we must intentionally relate to people in accessible ways, but this does not mean that we should dumb everything down to be appealing and then not try to lift worshipers beyond the lowest common denominator. As Os Guinness insists, it is "perfectly legitimate" to "convey the gospel in cartoons to a nonliterary generation incapable of rising above MTV. . . . But five years later, if the new disciples are truly won to Christ, they will be reading Paul's letter to the Romans."[4]

Precisely. We must meet worshipers where they are and try to lift them higher. But Dawn offers no suggestions as to how we should "intentionally relate to people in accessible ways," except perhaps Guinness's "gospel in cartoons." One obvious possible solution is that we teachers should humble ourselves to accept the help that CWM can provide. Dawn is evidently not willing to give CWM even this much credit. But fair-minded readers should find it obvious that CWM can play a valuable role even in the intellectual task we call teaching.

But I would not want to leave readers with the impression that CWM is intellectually valuable only for unbelieving visitors and spiritual babies. Recall my point in chapter 3 that CWM is an excellent medium for communicating biblical content in a fresh and vivid way, especially (but not exclusively) to younger people. We all need to learn God's Word. As I mentioned, my congregation would not know and treasure Revelation 15:3–4 if it were not for a Scripture song based on that text. So we see that CWM can play a valuable role in teaching people at all stages of their spiritual growth.

At one point, Dawn recommends the traditional liturgy because it helps children and adults in committing Christian truth to memory. Her discussion is a good one, but there is no positive mention of CWM, only a complaint that in "many" contemporary services the children do not get involved. If she really thinks there are no CWM songs accessible to children, then I must repeat my earlier suspicion that she does not know CWM. In fact, many CWM songs are excellent vehicles for getting God's Word into the memories of worshipers—both adults and children. Yes, memorizing God's Word is a worthy goal of worship. Why can't Dawn concede the obvious point that CWM songs can be a useful means to such memorization?

And, dare I say it? CWM can even lead us into areas of intellectual profundity: First, because it scriptural, and God's Word is always profound. God's Word edifies the young and the foolish; but the mature will never outgrow it. We can never exhaust the riches of revelation. Second, because it enables us to meditate on that truth. Traditional hymns tend to be longer than CWM songs, and their greatest advantage is theological richness. At their best, they say a lot. Consider for example, Charles Wesley's "Arise, My Soul, Arise," a fine traditional hymn.

> Arise, my soul, arise, shake off thy guilty fears:
> The bleeding sacrifice in my behalf appears:
> Before the Throne my Surety stands,
> Before the Throne my Surety stands,
> My name is written on his hands.

Wonderful theology here, but there is so much of it, and it goes by so quickly! (1) We should not fear God's wrath (2) because Jesus has sacrificed himself for our sins, and (3) because he is our "surety," guaranteeing our acceptance with God, and (4) because he stands before the Father's throne, pleading on our behalf. (5) Our names are written on his hands—we are identified with Christ so that God accepts us in him. Then come the other three stanzas: (6) Jesus is resurrected and lives forever in heaven, so (7) he will never stop interceding for us. (8) His love is great to redeem us by his blood. (9) His wounds therefore plead for us. Therefore, (10) God the Father is reconciled to us. (11) He speaks the assuring word that we are forgiven. (12) He adopts us as his children. (13) In consideration of the above, we find we can no longer fear. (14) So we draw near to God in confidence. (15) And we address him as "Abba, Father."

Any of these fifteen points could constitute the subject matter of a sermon, even a series of sermons. Although it is a good teaching hymn, it is not easily remembered. I have sung it a hundred times or so, and I still have to open the hymnal to get the words right. The traditional tunes used for the hymn are not much help. None of them, in my judgment, is a very good means to impress these truths on the hearts of modern worshipers.

A good CWM song in the same doctrinal area typically would focus on *one* of the fifteen points, surround it with hallelujahs, show how that point should matter to the singers, set it to a memorable tune, and give people some time to meditate on the wonder of that biblical teaching. For example, consider "Father God, I Wonder," by Ian Smale, which focuses on the doctrine of adoption (points 12 and 15 above):

> Father God, I wonder how I managed to exist
> Without the knowledge of Your parenthood and Your
>   loving care.
> But now I am Your son, I am adopted in your family,
> And I can never be alone,
> 'Cause, Father God, You're there beside me.
>
> I will sing your praises,
> I will sing your praises,
> I will sing your praises forever more. [Repeat.][5]

Now a superficial evaluation will conclude that Wesley's hymn has far more intellectual "content" and "depth" than Smale's, and therefore that it is far more worthy of inclusion in worship. In one sense, certainly, Wesley's hymn does have more content and depth. But recall that in worship we should not be interested in intellect for intellect's sake. Rather, we want intellectual content for the purpose of teaching. And it is certainly not immediately obvious that Wesley's hymn is a better teaching tool than Smale's. Wesley's hymn covers far more material. But I am not at all sure that it is as effective as Smale's in communicating that content to modern worshipers.[6]

My conclusion is not that we should drop traditional hymnody. "Arise, My Soul, Arise" is edifying in its way, particularly to more mature Christians. It is good to become aware in some measure as to how all those doctrines fit together, and to praise God for the very richness of our salvation. But Smale's hymn may very well be more helpful to more people today in bringing them to a higher level of understanding.

Therefore, though it may sound strange to say it, the intellectual function of worship is one of the best arguments in favor of CWM, as long as we understand that intellectual function scripturally rather than from the standpoint of the secular academy. We should guard the intellectual quality of worship, not because we want to cater to the academic elite; nor to atone for the anti-intellectualism of past generations; nor because of the "primacy of the intellect"; nor because the intellectual elements of Scripture are somehow more important to worship than the emotional or volitional elements; nor because abstract, complex, technical, or difficult language is somehow good in itself. Rather, we should treasure the intellectual substance of worship because in it God comes to teach us, to take away our ignorance and foolishness and fill us with the wisdom and knowledge of Jesus. And it is just that sort of teaching that CWM does very well.

Education is a complex business. You don't educate people by sticking something in front of their faces that they cannot presently understand. Nor, as Dawn rightly emphasizes, do you dumb down everything to the level of immediate accessibility without doing anything to help your student grow. You educate by using tools that will address the student where he is and gently lead him to greater understanding. Seen in that way, CWM can be a good tool of education. In that sense we may say that CWM is highly intellectual!

The problem is that each congregation contains worshipers who are on many different levels of maturity and knowledge. It is not easy to edify them all in worship, but we must try. There should be songs for both young and mature Christians, some songs that are relatively simple and some that are relatively complex. Scripture warrants this sort of variety—compare Psalm 133 to Psalm 68. And both the young and the mature must bear with one another in love, rather than demanding their own aesthetic or intellectual preferences. That humble spirit is part of what we are to teach. It is the mind of Christ (Phil. 2:5). If we look at the worship of the church from this perspective, I do not see how we can deny the value of CWM (or, indeed, of traditional hymnody) within the teaching ministry of the church.

Worship as Personal Encounter

In the above discussion, I have been focusing on the teaching function of worship, trying to show that even in the most intellectual aspects of worship, CWM can play a positive role. But I wish to stress here that there is more to worship than teaching. Worship is not merely an educational experience; it is first of all a meeting between ourselves and God. Teaching is one thing God does for us in these meetings. But he also relates to us in all the rich and complicated ways that a loving father relates to his children. Worship is an exchange of love, comfort, peace, encouragement, challenge, and many other things. In these areas, CWM has even more obvious benefits than in the area of teaching.

Think for a minute how you would respond if God actually appeared to you, right now, wherever you are. If you could bring yourself to speak, what would you say? Job planned a speech to make before God, demanding that God answer his questions (Job 23:1–7; 31:35ff.). But when God actually met him, God asked the questions; Job put his hand over his mouth (Job 40:4–5). I suspect that if God were to appear to you or me as he appeared to Moses (Ex. 3) or Isaiah, we too would forget our planned speeches and respond to God very simply indeed. Most likely we would cry out for forgiveness, as did Isaiah (Isa. 6) and Job (42:3–6). Beyond that, we would likely utter some very simple praises or thanksgivings—something like CWM. This is how the glorified saints and angels worship in heaven (Rev. 4:11; 5:9–14; 11:15–18; etc.).

There are times in our worship where it is important to recognize that although God is invisible, he is just as present to us as he was to Moses, Job, and Isaiah. At those times, transfer of new and difficult concepts does not take the first priority. These are times when we speak to God as the children we are. For these are times in which we learn one of the greatest lessons of our Christian education—that God's thoughts are not our thoughts and his ways not our ways (Isa. 55:8). At those times, I believe, CWM can say more than any other kind of hymnody available to us.

I fear that this dimension of worship needs to be recovered in Reformed churches. We should not be so defensive of our intellectual achievements, or so persuaded of such dogmas as the "primacy of the intellect," that we are unable simply to rest in the arms of our gracious, loving Lord. Contrary to Ulrich Zwingli, worship does not always have to be a seminar. It can also be a reassurance that God's love is greater than anything we can calculate (Eph. 3:17–19), a love that surpasses knowledge.

Notes

1. On these points, see my *Doctrine of the Knowledge of God* (Phillipsburg, N.J.: Presbyterian and Reformed, 1987).

2. For Marva Dawn's analysis of this question and my response, see appendix 1.

3. See my *Doctrine of the Knowledge of God,* especially 328–46.

4. Marva Dawn, *Reaching Out Without Dumbing Down* (Grand Rapids: Eerdmans, 1995), 125.

5. MMPCB, 114.

6. The confusion between "teaching" and merely "covering material" exists in many areas of the church's ministry, including preaching and Christian education. The teaching ministry of the church is often hindered by failure to understand that distinction.

CHAPTER 10

❧

Quality

One of the major concerns about CWM is that the music and texts are not of "high quality." This question is related to those discussed in the previous several chapters, but it has broader ramifications. Many critics believe that CWM songs are of poor quality, unworthy to bring before God in worship.

Different Kinds of Quality

It would be easy to dismiss this whole issue as a matter of taste, but I don't intend to do that. I am not an aesthetic or musical relativist. Some music is certainly better, aesthetically speaking, than other music, and some hymn texts are better than other texts. Generally speaking, the music of J. S. Bach is better than that of Lowell Mason, and the texts of Isaac Watts are superior to those of Philip Bliss. Scripture itself speaks highly of the "skillfulness" of the temple instrumentalists, singers, and craftsmen (1 Chron. 15:22; 28:21; Ps. 33:3), indicating that God does care about quality. Certainly if our praises are sacrifices (Heb. 13:15; cf. Hos. 14:2), they should be of the first fruits, the best that we have.

Of course, quality is not an affair of simple perception, like perceiving the blue of the sky. People do disagree about it, and their differences are influenced by various sorts of presuppositions, especially once they get beyond obvious comparisons such as that between Bach and Mason. So although there is such a thing as objective quality, it is possible for knowledgeable and godly people to differ as to what constitutes quality in a particular instance.

Further, it is plain that quality in the abstract is not a sufficient criterion for the choice of hymns in worship. In the abstract, one can picture quality as something measured precisely by degrees, so that some particular song would be of a higher quality than all the others—or perhaps several songs would be tied for "first place" in quality. We might say, for the sake of argument, that "A Mighty Fortress" is the best hymn ever written. Then singing anything else would involve a decrease in quality. The conclusion, then, would be that we should never sing anything other than "A Mighty Fortress," because any other hymn would be less than "the best." Then the best way of planning worship would be to find the best hymn(s) ever written and then sing them over and over again.

That would be wrong, for the following reasons: (1) Hymns achieving such first-place status would doubtless be few, and their exclusive use would be dull and tiresome to a congregation. Even the highest quality music, even "A Mighty Fortress," can become routine after many consecutive hearings. (2) Probably such first-place hymns would not be adequate to communicate all the rich and varied subject matter of Scripture. So for at least these two reasons, we must be willing to supplement the "best" hymns with relatively "inferior" hymns. There are, in other words, times and situations where quality as an abstract concept must and should be overridden by other considerations. The fact that hymn A is musically and textually superior to hymn B doesn't imply that we must always prefer A over B.

The worship literature abounds in exhortations to bring before God "only the best."[1] I have declared above my agreement with that basic idea. But we should not place an absurdly literal interpretation on the word "best." In this context, best simply means music that is generally excellent and adequate for its purpose.

The mention of "purpose" reminds us that there are different *kinds* of quality. The aesthetic skillfulness evident in a hymn is not the only kind of quality relevant to worship. For example, discussions of quality in music often exclude the important question of the quality of communication. But as we've seen, communication is one of the most important considerations in worship. A Bach chorale in German may have an excellent tune, a wonderful harmonization, and a profound text; but because it is in German it would likely not be useful in an English-speaking worship service.[2] In that context it would not be the "best" choice.

In planning worship for our time, it is, of course, important to choose music that communicates with contemporary people. Marva Dawn insists that music is not excellent enough for worship unless it is "great enough to be preserved beyond its own time."[3] Although I appreciate the impulse behind this statement, I do not literally agree with it. There may very well be music that serves very well to communicate God's Word to people of our own time which, nevertheless, will rightly be discarded by future generations. I believe that we may sacrifice endurability to achieve communication, if that communication itself is truly excellent.

I recommend CWM songs not because they are of better aesthetic quality than Bach chorales but because many are excellent—high quality—means of communicating the Word of God in some settings. And, although they don't achieve historically first-place levels of musical and textual quality, nevertheless, the better ones are far from bad, and in many cases they are better than many traditional hymns.

Is CWM Postmodern?

I would now like to examine some critical approaches to CWM that question the quality of the songs. Reminiscent of our earlier discussions of whether CWM was too closely related to the negative trends of modern culture, Daryl Hart argues that CWM is "postmodern" in the sense that it rejects the very notion that there are any standards of good and bad to be applied to worship.

Postmodernism is an odd concept. As William Edgar asks, how

can anything be *post*modern?[4] But this term has become a conventional designation for certain trends in recent thought and culture. Dawn finds that the most common form of postmodernism rejects authority to the point of nihilism, denies objective knowledge, and relativistically affirms an indefinite number of points of view. She comments,

> A baseball joke makes clear the progression in history from the premodern belief in objective truth to postmodernity's deconstructionism. A premodern umpire once said, "There's balls and there's strikes, and I calls 'em as they is." Believing in an absolute truth that could be found, earlier societies looked for evidence to discover that truth. A modern umpire would say instead, "There's balls and there's strikes, and I calls 'em as I sees 'em." For the modernist, truth is to be found in one's own experience. Now a postmodern umpire would say, "There's balls and there's strikes, and they ain't nothin' till I calls 'em." No truth exists unless we create it.[5]

Dawn doesn't say anything specific about postmodernism in relation to CWM. Her concerns about postmodernism melt into her general line of argument. But Hart has raised the issue of postmodernism very specifically in relation to CWM.

His article "Post-modern Evangelical Worship" is found among the "Scholia" of the *Calvin Theological Journal*.[6] There are no footnotes or bibliography, though there are a few undocumented references and quotations, and Hart refers to only one or two CWM songs (he calls them P&W for "praise and worship"). I gather, therefore, that in this generally scholarly journal, "scholia" are articles not intended to be scholarly but merely to express some scholar's off-hand opinions. Like Dawn, Hart obviously has little firsthand knowledge of the CWM literature. So in some respects, his diatribe scarcely deserves serious attention. But it does express vividly the alleged parallel between CWM and postmodernism, and so I will reflect upon it here briefly.

He begins by asking the provocative question, "What do Billy

Graham and Stanley Fish have in common?" Fish, a professor of English at Duke University, is a high priest of postmodernism. Evangelicals like Billy Graham, says Hart, have the reputation of being on the opposite side of the fence from the postmodernists. They are part of a movement that "defends the traditional family, opposes political correctness and multiculturalism in the academy, and supports efforts to cut federal funding for objectionable art."[7]

"Why is it then," he asks, "that when evangelicals retreat from the public square into their houses of worship they manifest the same hostility to tradition, intellectual standards, and good taste they find so deplorable in their opponents in the culture wars?"[8] The villain is P&W or CWM.

In both postmodernism and contemporary worship, "we see a form of anti-elitism that questions any distinction between good and bad (or even not so good), or between what is appropriate or inappropriate."[9] The result is that in all the P&W literature, there is no "adequate expression of the historic truths of the faith."[10] P&W is radically individualist, and that is devastating. "For the idea that the autonomous individual must find his own meaning or experience or reality for himself ends up making such individuals unwilling to follow and submit to the forms, habits, and standards that have guided a community or culture."[11]

These evangelicals share with the postmodernists "an inability to see the value of restraint, habit, and form."[12] They fail to see that

> the traditions that Presbyterians follow, for instance, are not done to throttle religious experience but rather, as the prescribed means of communing with God and his people . . . Presbyterians have conducted public and family worship in specific ways because they believe that worship should conform to God's revealed truth.[13]

Without these traditions, in P&W "the service and elements are designed to attract attention themselves rather than functioning as vehicles for expressing adoration to God."[14] Rather than worshiping God, they may well be "worshiping their emotions."[15] Thus "this commitment to making the gospel accessible deforms and trivializes Christianity, making it no better than any other commodity exchanged on the market."[16]

Some of these issues we have discussed already, such as the issues of self-centered individualism, intellectual standards, the marketing mentality, and doctrinal orthodoxy. Others we shall discuss later, such as the importance of tradition. But our concern here is whether CWM is a mere creature of contemporary culture, selling out its Christian heritage for a trendy relativism. A few comments:

(1) Hart offers no evidence for his accusation that advocates of contemporary worship "question any distinction between good or bad . . . appropriate or inappropriate." Among CWM worship leaders, there are just as many discussions about quality and appropriateness as among planners of traditional services. That the CWM leaders reach different conclusions from Hart does not prove that they have no standards at all.

(2) If some CWM advocates are anti-elitist, some traditionalists are undoubtedly elitist. The fact that postmodernists are anti-elitist does not imply that we should all become elitists. But calling one another names won't help the discussion. The truth, I think, is somewhat as follows: It is wrong to govern worship either by the criterion of popularity or by the tastes of those who love high art and tradition. The goal in worship is to express the truth of God in forms marked by high quality as well as vivid and memorable communication. The balance of quality and communication is not easy to achieve. Advocates of CWM are often biased on the side of communication, while critics of it are biased on the side of quality in the abstract. Neither group is universally and always in the right.

(3) A similar point should be made in response to Hart's bewilderment over the shift from conservatism to liberalism when many evangelicals move from politics to worship. How can they be in favor of "traditional values" in the political arena and at the same time favor radical change in the area of worship? I question how radical CW and CWM really are; see the following chapter on that subject. But more important: The standard for evangelical churches must always be the Scriptures, not either conservatism

or liberalism in the abstract. Sometimes following Scripture makes us appear conservative in the context of society; sometimes it makes us appear liberal or radical. The important thing is that we follow God's Word no matter what people think.

(4) Are traditional forms "prescribed by God"? Are they the only legitimate way for worship to "conform to God's revealed truth"? Well, God has certainly prescribed that we do certain things in worship: praise, prayer, preaching, sacraments, and so on. But he has not prescribed that we do these things in precisely the way that Presbyterians have done them throughout their history. God does not prescribe that hymns use four part chordal harmony in stately rhythm. He does not prescribe organs instead of guitars. (Indeed, I think the instruments mentioned in the Psalm headings are more like guitars, trumpets, and drums than like organs.) He does not prescribe old music rather than new. He does not prescribe formal language rather than informal. There are many areas in which God's prescriptions allow freedom to choose from a range of options. The current discussion is not, I think, mostly about matters that God has actually prescribed; it is mostly about areas in which we are to make our own choices within the limits of the larger principles of Scripture.

(5) Hart's statement that in P&W "the service and elements are designed to attract attention themselves rather than functioning as vehicles for expressing adoration to God" is downright slanderous. How does he know the motives of those who design the services? And we have seen earlier in this book that CWM is a movement of God-centered worship that focuses on praise. As in Bruce Ballinger's "We Have Come into This House,"[17] it exhorts worshipers, "So forget about yourself, and concentrate on Him, and worship Him."

(6) Words like "deform" and "trivialize" are very serious terms in theological discussion. Normally to speak of deformed worship is to speak of alleged worship that is not worship at all. I hope that Hart doesn't mean to make such a strong point. But either his rhetoric has gotten away from him, or he is condemning a whole branch of the church of Jesus Christ for no good reason.

(7) Hart comes closest to the truth when he says that this

movement, like postmodernism, is skeptical of tradition. That point is important enough for us to examine at length in the next chapter. But even at this point we must raise a question. Adherence to tradition admits of different forms and degrees. To the Roman Catholic Church, the Protestant Reformers were anti-traditional. Within Protestantism today, there is a continuum of traditionalism and anti-traditionalism that runs from Anglo-Catholicism on the one hand to the Plymouth Brethren on the other. (And even Plymouth Brethren do many things that Christians have traditionally done over the centuries.) I take it that Hart is not asking us to become Roman Catholic or Anglo-Catholic. But then which of the many degrees and kinds of traditionalism is he urging upon us? If he cannot make the case that *any* departure from tradition "deforms and trivializes Christianity," what case can he make that only some precise *degree* of departure deforms and trivializes Christianity? And how could he argue that CWM is postmodern because it is guilty of that precise degree of departure? Is it that Presbyterians, perhaps, have it perfectly right and other Christians have it wrong? Well, which Presbyterians?

I confess that I find Hart's critique of contemporary worship utterly uninformed and unpersuasive. CWM is not postmodern in any meaningful sense. Hart makes the same methodological mistake as many others.[18] He sketches a movement in contemporary culture, assumes without any serious study or argument that CWM arises out of that movement, and then presents a distorted description of CWM to make it fit his concept of that movement. Further, he presents an equally distorted concept of Christian orthodoxy, derived not from the Scriptures, but from a *via negativa:* He redefines Christianity by making it at every point the opposite of the movement he opposes.

In my preface, I indicated that our study of CWM and its critics would unearth some deeper issues about the theological methods currently employed by evangelical and Reformed theologians. Although I seriously intend this book to be a defense of CWM, I have another major purpose as well in this book: to call into question the theological method I have just described. I am convinced that this is a very serious issue. This approach to theological criticism and evaluation is quite widespread and is practiced by some of the most respected evangelical theologians on other issues, as well as this one. It is unscriptural and divisive, and leads to distorted conclusions.

Quality and the Critics

If the critics of CWM are united on anything, they are one in their judgment that CWM is uniformly low in quality. Hart speaks of contemporary worship as evidencing a "hostility to tradition, intellectual standards, and good taste."[19] He says,

> It is virtually impossible to make the case—without having your hearers go glassy-eyed—that "Of the Father's Love Begotten" is a better text than "Shine, Jesus, Shine," and, therefore, that the former is fitting for corporate worship, while the latter should remain confined to Christian radio.[20]

We discussed earlier the question of whether CWM observes any standards of good and bad, and I argued that it does. But are those standards adequate? What kind of standards are operating when "Shine, Jesus, Shine" replaces "Of the Father's Love Begotten"?

The quotation from Hart displays, I think, what I earlier described as an *abstract* notion of quality. Let us grant that "Of the Father's Love" is a "better" text than "Shine, Jesus, Shine." Does that imply that the latter should be "confined to Christian radio"? Well, to return to our previous example, I happen to believe that "A Mighty Fortress Is Our God" is a better text in most relevant respects than "Fairest Lord Jesus." Does that imply that the latter hymn "should be confined to Christian radio"?[21] If, as earlier, we assume for the sake of argument that "A Mighty Fortress" is the greatest hymn ever written, is it then the only hymn that should not be relegated to Christian radio?

You see, "quality" in the abstract is not an appropriate measure of church music. But we may surely evaluate hymns by determining how well they communicate the Word of God to particular worshipers. On that criterion, I believe that "Shine, Jesus, Shine," stands up pretty well against "Of the Father's Love Begotten." Indeed, I think that Hart's example furnishes us with a useful test case for further examination.

"Of the Father's Love Begotten" is certainly a great hymn by objective measurement. It has stood the test of time, ascribed to Aurelius Clemens Prudentius (348–413) and translated into English by John Mason Neale in the nineteenth century. The first stanza reads,

> Of the Father's love begotten
> 　ere the worlds began to be,
> He is Alpha and Omega, He the source, the ending he,
> Of the things that are, that have been,
> 　and that future years shall see.

(Some settings add, as a refrain, "ever more and ever more, Amen" after each stanza.) This verse speaks of Jesus' eternal Trinitarian generation and pre-existence, and of his being both origin and goal of all existence through time. These are wonderful biblical truths, but certainly not easily accessible to theologically unsophisticated worshipers. The language does not help much: the archaism "ere," the chiastic but unusual "He the source, the ending he." If any worshiper is unfamiliar with these ideas and this hymn, the stanza goes by far too quickly to make much sense. Like Charles Wesley's "Arise, My Soul, Arise," which I examined earlier, this hymn is rich in theological ideas, but it piles them on very quickly, giving no time for reflection or meditation. One who knows about Jesus' eternal generation and who has sung the hymn before will appreciate this text as a means of summing up the doctrine with poetic conciseness. But for the majority of worshipers who have not reached this point of maturity, the hymn states too many deep doctrines too fast to be truly edifying.

In this respect, the second stanza is somewhat an improvement. It stays with one theme, the expectation of Jesus by prophets before his birth. But who were the "heav'n taught singers"? When did they "sing of old with one accord"?

Verses 3–5 are a kind of ancient praise song. They call everything in heaven and earth to praise the Trinitarian God, as does the traditional doxology. They are fine, though some poetry is awkward. For example,

> Thee let age and thee let manhood,
> Thee let boys in chorus sing.

The first line is meaningless without the second, which either loses the attention of worshipers or sets them on a course of trying to figure it out, which they cannot accomplish in the time available. And what does it mean for age, manhood, and boys to sing "Thee" in chorus? The problems: (1) an archaic pronoun, (2) abstractions (age and manhood) being coordinated with concrete persons (boys, and later matrons, virgins, maidens), (3) the use of "Thee" as a direct object to "sing": we know what it means to sing a song, or sing a truth, but it is not immediately obvious what it means to sing a person. The ideas in these verses can be found in many CWM songs, and arguably the CWM songs impress these truths more clearly and vividly upon the modern worshiper.

There are two tunes commonly used with this text. One is a twelfth-century plainsong, "Divinum Mysterium," which is almost impossible to teach in a congregation not otherwise accustomed to chanting. The other is John Goss's "Praise My Soul," an exceptionally good piece of music, in my opinion. (I particularly like the harmonic progression in the third and fourth lines, building toward the dominant, then returning immediately to the tonic for the fifth line.) It is, however, not as appropriate as "Divinum Mysterium" to express the great mysteries of the eternal generation of Jesus. Its marching rhythm seems somehow too matter-of-fact. And it is very much a traditional hymn-setting, and therefore its power of communication is largely directed to fairly mature Christians.

These problems are not major in my view, and I would not hesitate on their account to use this hymn in contemporary worship. I only wish to point out that, conceived as a means of driving home biblical truth to people of our time, this hymn is not a perfect vehicle. Therefore it, and hymns like it, need to be supplemented with other hymns that are more immediately accessible to modern worshipers.

Now "Shine, Jesus, Shine":[22] For some reason, more than one critic of CWM has picked out this song as a symbol of all that is wrong with its musical genre. I'm not sure why. I suspect that the critics are attracted to it because they perceive its title as banal and perhaps irreverent, especially since this line is coupled in the chorus with "blaze, Spirit, blaze" and "flow, river, flow." I do not, however, think this is a very good example to serve the critics' purposes. Indeed, I can think of many other CWM songs that make better "horrible examples" than this one. Actually, when you look closely at "Shine, Jesus, Shine," you should see that it is rather good.

This song is written by Graham Kendrick, who of all the contributors to MMPCB is probably most like a composer of traditional hymns. "Shine, Jesus, Shine" is in three stanzas with a chorus. Its theme is Jesus as the light of the world, one of many ideas concisely addressed in "Of the Father's Love." Toward the end of verse 2 of the latter hymn, we hear the phrase "Now he shines, the long expected." No explanation or reflection. An intelligent but theologically uninformed worshiper might ask, "Why does the hymn speak of Jesus *shining?*" Well, Kendrick's hymn answers that question. It is a typical CWM song in that it focuses on one truth rather than trying to cover a wide range of theological encyclopedia. But it is atypical in that it relates that truth to many others in Scripture. Here are the hymn stanzas:

> Lord, the light of Your love is shining
> In the midst of the darkness shining;
> Jesus, Light of the World, shine upon us,
> Set us free by the truth You now bring us,
> Shine on me, shine on me.
>
> Lord, I come to Your awesome presence,
> From the shadows into your radiance;

By the blood I may enter Your brightness,
Search me, try me, consume all my darkness,
Shine on me, shine on me.

As we gaze on your Kingly brightness,
So our faces display Your likeness;
Ever changing from glory to glory,
Mirror'd here may our lives tell Your story,
Shine on me, shine on me.

The quality of the poetry is certainly not objectionable. Notice that the three stanzas proceed through the offices of Christ as prophet ("set us free by the truth"), priest ("by the blood I may enter Your brightness"), and king ("As we gaze on your kingly brightness"). We can also read this text in terms of John 14:6: Jesus is the way (stanza 2), the truth (stanza 1), and the life (stanza 3). The two triads are closely related, of course. Kendrick doesn't shout this schema at us; he just uses it, leaving us with the sense of a genuinely biblical and traditional (!) progression of thought.

The text focuses on Jesus as light of the world, gathering together a number of scriptural expressions of that theme: the light as truth, the light as God's righteousness over against our sin, the light as God's very nature reflected in us as his image. Someone who shares David Wells's critique of evangelical anti-intellectualism should rejoice in this song's affirmation that Jesus sets us free by his truth. Those who like Historicus think that CWM never mentions the "conditions of entrance into God's presence" should rejoice that this song speaks of entering God's presence by the truth of Christ (verse 1) and by his shed blood (verse 2). Verse three also refutes Historicus's contention that CWM never speaks of the life-changing consequences of salvation.

The tune, too, is better than most. The verse tune is really quite fascinating. It begins on the fifth of the scale (E in the key of A Major) rather than the tonic, giving us a sense of being in the middle of things. Then the tune works its way gradually, through ups and downs, toward the upper tonic, but it never quite reaches that goal. The harmonic progression is creative. In the line "Jesus, light of the world" it advances to the dominant E chord, but then instead of resolving to the tonic goes to C# minor and F# minor, holding back our hope of resolution. That resolution comes, of course, in the chorus, where the A Major tonality is reestablished decisively.

I am less enthusiastic about the chorus, both music and text. Although the tune of the chorus does provide a triumphant resolution of the musical tensions in the verse, it is not nearly as interesting as what has gone before. The four lines all begin with the same seven-note phrase, which to me comes across as somewhat monotonous.

The text of the refrain, with "Shine, Jesus, Shine" and "Blaze, Spirit, Blaze," seems a bit much. Some might be uneasy that the text addresses Christ and the Spirit with imperatives, in effect telling them to do something. But that kind of language is scriptural, as in Psalm 94:1–2:

> O LORD, the God who avenges,
>   O God who avenges, shine forth.
> Rise up, O Judge of the earth;
>   pay back to the proud what they deserve.

(Note the term "shine" in the second line.) It just seems to me that to sing this through three times tries the patience of worshipers too much. But perhaps I am just venting my own emotions at this point. For most worshipers, I think, the chorus rather rollicks along, supplying the needed climax, carrying worshipers with it, rendering most criticisms beside the point.

My general verdict is that the verse of this song is really outstanding, in verbal and musical content. The chorus is less valuable. But the verse lines need something to supply a climax for the longing expressed, to supply an "already" in response to the "not yet." Kendrick's chorus does serve that need acceptably. All in all, the hymn is above average among others written through the history of hymnody. Would I ever use it in preference to "Of the Father's Love?" Yes. I believe that "Shine, Jesus, Shine," is a generally excellent hymn and that in general it communicates better with modern worshipers than "Of the Father's Love."

But if I were trying seriously to teach my congregation the doctrine of Christ's eternal generation, I would take pains to teach them, and explain, "Of the Father's Love."

I doubt that Hart has actually read the words to "Shine, Jesus, Shine." Certainly the comparison between that song and "Of the Father's Love" is not a slam dunk in favor of the latter, and I find it hard to understand why Hart should think that it is, unless his judgment arises from carelessness. I would again urge critics to become far more familiar with the pieces they criticize.

Repetition

I should perhaps also address one specific issue in regard to quality. CWM songs are notorious among the critics for being too repetitious. Hart refers to the traditional joke-description of CWM songs: "four words, three notes and two hours."[23]

There are two kinds of repetition in CWM songs: first, repetition in the number of times a song is sung, and second, repetition within the song itself. To consider the first: There is a tradition in charismatic circles to sing a short song over and over again, for perhaps ten or twenty minutes. I once attended a conference for worship leaders in which we sang "I Love You, Lord"[24] over and over again for maybe twenty minutes. It was an unforgettable experience. The worship leader asked us to sing while meditating on different themes, while praying about various matters. We sang some stanzas on our knees, some standing, some with arms raised. Sometimes we listened while the pianist improvised on the theme. In other words, there was a lot going on. We didn't just sing, but we did many other things as well. My own testimony was that it was quite a challenging spiritual exercise.[25] I don't think I'd want to do it at every worship service; it could easily lose its power to focus my attention on God. But on that one occasion, this exercise did enable me to focus on the greatness and mercy of the Lord.

We don't do that in our own congregation. Our rule is to sing multi-stanza hymns once, single-stanza hymns twice. That seems enough for us as a general rule, but I can understand why that would not be sufficient for other congregations. Each congregation must, I think, make reasonable judgments about how much repetition is truly edifying and how much is merely tiresome. And if singing a song three times is tiresome, the answer is instead to sing it twice or once.

Considering the second kind of repetition, repetition within the songs themselves, will help us to think about the very nature of repetition and what it can do for us in worship. Elsewhere in this book I have objected to intellectualist or academic models of worship. Now in most college- or graduate-level liberal arts and science courses, repetition is typically avoided. When a student attends a Tuesday lecture on the history of England, let's say, he or she does not normally expect to hear the same lecture at the Wednesday class. The chief object in such lectures is the communication of information. The professor communicates the lecture on Tuesday, and it goes into the students' notes. Thereafter, it doesn't need to be given again. Of course, even in academic contexts, repetition is not entirely forbidden. Most educators understand that repetition is a valuable tool for teaching children. And skillful lecturers, even in college and graduate school, understand how to underscore basic themes through repetition, while not, of course, repeating everything ad nauseam.

In other forms of communication, however, repetition plays a much larger role. I told my future wife "I love you," during our courtship. But if I never said it again for the twelve years of our marriage, Mary would certainly have a legitimate complaint against me. Love is not like academic information. It is not something you can express once and then consider it done. The communication of human love is not once-for-all. It calls for repetition, amplification, translation into many variants. Our lovers do not just want to hear "I love you"; they want to hear "I love you, I love you, I love you!"

Political allegiance is similar. I remember a cartoon from some years ago, where all the children in a classroom are pledging allegiance to the flag except one girl. As the teacher scowls at her, she replies, "I pledged allegiance yesterday." The girl did not understand that loyalty to flag and country is something that must be reaffirmed regularly, not settled once-for-all.

In these respects, worship is far more like love and loyalty than like college lectures. It is not only communication of information (though it is that), but communication of love and fidelity. Our relationship to God is that of a bride to a husband, and like that of a servant to a king. The church is both God's family and his covenant nation. Therefore in worship we reaffirm both our love and our loyalty.

Surely it is not enough to do this once. That is why we meet over and over again, Sunday after Sunday. And the language of worship that we use each Sunday is, even in the most traditional services, richly repetitious. "Hallelujah" occurs in the Psalms over and over again. In the Psalms, the same themes keep recurring: God is my rock, my trust, my shield. Deliver me from my enemics, O Lord. Let me not be put to shame. Why have you not delivered me? But I will wait on the Lord and he will answer. . . . These repetitions occur from psalm to psalm, and even within psalms. Indeed, the chief characteristic of Hebrew poetry is parallelism of ideas: the psalmist says something, then says the same thing again a bit differently. Or he says something and then states a contrasting truth. Some psalms are arranged chiastically, so that the first idea is repeated in the sixth, the second in the fifth, the third in the fourth, and so on.

Why, we wonder, do the seraphs in Isaiah 6 say "Holy" three times? Wouldn't once or twice have been enough? The living creatures in Revelation 4:8 are even more persistent: "Day and night they never stop saying "Holy, holy, holy is the Lord God Almighty, who was, and is, and is to come." Elsewhere, Scripture urges such persistence upon us:

> I will extol the LORD at all times;
>   his praise will always [KJV: continually] be on my lips.
>   (Ps. 34:1; cf. 35:27)

> Sing to the LORD, praise his name;
>   proclaim his salvation day after day. (Ps. 96:2)

Our prayers, too, are to be constant and persistent (Acts 1:14; 6:4; Col. 4:2; 1 Thess. 5:17; 1 Tim. 5:5).

As the language of love says "I love you, I love you, I love you!" so the language of worship is "Holy, holy, holy is the Lord! We praise you! We praise you! We praise you!"

Traditional liturgy is repetitious; indeed it is often criticized as too much so. It tends to be repetitious from week to week, while CWM tends to employ repetition within each song. Should we be distressed about that? I think not in any general way. Certainly in the light of the biblical passages noted above, we cannot object to repetition as such. Obviously there are some limits, but those limits must be worked out in the concrete, not in the abstract. If a particular song contains so many repetitions that it distracts our attention from the worship of God, then that song should be rewritten or not used. My own perception, however, is that if we abandon abstract objections to repetition, we will not find most CWM songs overly repetitious.

What, then, does Jesus mean by *vain* repetition in Matthew 6:7? The NIV translates his words, "And when you pray, do not keep on babbling like pagans, for they think they will be heard because of their many words. Do not be like them, because your Father knows what you need before you ask him" (Matt. 6:7–8). Some thoughts: (1) This passage is dealing with petitionary prayer, which is rather different from the activities of praise and teaching. (2) These verses cannot be taken to condemn what Scripture elsewhere provides for us: repetitive praise and teaching. (3) In this passage Jesus focuses on the motives of the pagan "babblers." They deny God's sovereign knowledge of our needs, and they think God will hear them because of the sheer quantity of their words. That is a danger in CW and all forms of worship. But I don't believe it is a special problem in CW or CWM.

Dawn's objections to hymns that "sing over and over again only that God loves us" are somewhat curious. Why should the Taizé songs be commended for "constant repetition of one attribute of God" while CWM songs are condemned for repeating God's attribute of love? Is love the only attribute of God that we cannot praise over and over again?

And in fact, if MMPCB is any guide, there aren't very many CWM songs that actually speak over and over again of God's love. The index lists eleven songs under the entry, "God, love of." (By way of comparison, there are twenty-five songs under "God, majesty of.") Of the songs about love, five are settings of Scripture texts. One is "Shine, Jesus, Shine," which, as we have seen, speaks of many things besides love. In others, "He Is Faithful," "He Is Our Peace," "Like a River," love is one theme, balanced by others. Of this group of songs, the one in which love is most central is "Oh, How He Loves You and Me," by Kurt Kaiser,[26] which contains the line, "He gave his life, what more could he give?" So the song is not about some vague kind of love, but love defined in terms of the atonement, as is common in the New Testament (John 3:16; 15:13–14; Rom. 5:8; 1 John 4:9–10).

I realize of course that there are many misunderstandings abroad about God's love. Dawn is right that teaching about the love of God must be put in the context of his other attributes, human sin, atonement, and so on. We discussed earlier the importance of context. But there are many ways of presenting that context. We should not assume that because context is important, we should use only hymns that cover large amounts of doctrinal territory, thus eliminating at the outset any simple, childlike hymns. We can supply the context by using songs about God's love, and in the same service teaching the biblical context of love. Or by singing songs about love and also singing songs about other things.

Some Problems in CWM

We cannot, of course, analyze every CWM song to determine its quality in comparison to other CWM songs and to traditional hymnody. It should be evident, however, that such an investigation should not proceed on the assumption of abstract concepts of quality.

I do not claim that CWM songs are uniformly high in quality. Indeed, I think that many of them are undistinguished, even dull. And I have said that probably there are more dull songs in the

CWM literature than in most other hymn styles, simply because CWM has not undergone as much of the winnowing that takes place over time. Nevertheless, there are also some gems. In chapter 12, I will present my own song book, in which I will list some songs that seem to me to represent high quality in words and music. Readers, then, can make their own judgment. I do not, however, believe that the critics have made their general case against CWM. Their criticisms are based on invalid assumptions and personal feelings that should not go unquestioned.

But the CWM movement does need fair critics, who try to press the songwriters toward genuine improvement. The following are some of my own criticisms:

(1) The CWM movement greatly needs songwriters who will produce more thoughtful texts and excellent music.

(2) CWM needs greater doctrinal coverage. It deals excellently with topics such as praise, divine attributes, names of Jesus, the person and work of Christ, and the church as God's family. But other topics are not covered as well. CWM songwriters should create more songs especially on the subjects of the Word of God, creation, providence, humanity as God's image, sin, the Fall, the Resurrection, predestination, effectual calling, regeneration, saving faith, justification, sanctification, and the return of Christ. There are CWM songs on all these subjects, but not nearly enough.

(3) Worship leaders need to give more attention as to how CWM should function in worship. In chapter 5 I mentioned visiting a church in which the congregation listened passively to a praise team for twenty minutes. I do not believe that such periods of listening are always inappropriate to worship. But I do believe that God's people ought to spend a major amount of time participating actively, actually singing God's praise. In the church in question, we did not worship at all, except for listening to others worship. That service gave aid and comfort to the critics who claim that CWM is mere "entertainment." I believe that for the most part those critics are unfair; but they are not entirely wrong. Churches that use CWM need to give more thought to the theology of worship: what is worship according to Scripture?

(4) I have accused the CWM critics of speaking out of igno-

rance, careless thought, and prejudice, but that argument is two edged. For advocates of CWM have also often spoken unfairly and ignorantly about the traditional worship of the church. It is important for both sides to put away the flame throwers and speak to one another with the wisdom and love of Christ.

My concluding message for both advocates and critics of CWM is this: back to the Bible; *sola Scriptura*. If our major concern in worship is to follow Scripture, then we will be saved from both sterile traditionalism and unedifying innovation.

Notes

1. See, for example, Marva Dawn, *Reaching Out Without Dumbing Down* (Grand Rapids: Eerdmans, 1995), 202.

2. I recognize the possibility of commentary either orally or in a church bulletin to explain such a hymn. It may occasionally be useful to have an anthem in a foreign language and to explain the thrust of it to the worshipers. But that should not be the ordinary practice of worship.

3. Dawn, *Reaching Out*, 199.

4. William Edgar, "No News Is Good News: Modernity, the Postmodern, and Apologetics," *Westminster Theological Journal* 57 (Fall 1995), 359.

5. Dawn, *Reaching Out*, 36.

6. D. G. Hart, "Post-modern Evangelical Worship," *Calvin Theological Journal* 30 (1995), 451–59.

7. Ibid., 451.

8. Ibid.

9. Ibid., 452–53.

10. Ibid., 455.

11. Ibid., 456.

12. Ibid.

13. Ibid.

14. Ibid., 457. Does he mean "attract attention *to* themselves"?

15. Ibid., 458.

16. Ibid.

17. MMPCB, 204.

18. See appendix 2.

19. Hart, "Post-modern Evangelical Worship," 451.

20. Ibid., 453.

21. And, lest I get mail from Christian radio stations, let me also say that Hart here rather insults them. I do not believe that Christian radio should be, or that it usually is, a wastebasket for inferior music.

22. MMPCB, 2.

23. Hart, "Post-modern Evangelical Worship," 452. Marva Dawn also comments on the question of repetition. See appendix 1.

24. MMPCB, 21.

25. In appendix 1, I point out that there is more than one way of "exercising your spiritual muscles."

26. MMPCB, 238.

CHAPTER 11

❧

Tradition and Contemporaneity

I have often wondered why the theological establishment is so up in arms against CWM. As we have seen, CWM is the testimony of young Christians to God's grace in their lives. These songs are very close to the biblical text, focus on the praise of God, and communicate well with people of our time. It is hard to imagine why any knowledgeable Christian thinker would reject such music. But as we have seen, many do so out of ignorance of the songs and because of broader theological agendas wrongly applied to the CWM songs.

But why this remarkable carelessness in research and argumentation from people who are ordinarily intelligent and balanced in their theological judgment? And why do the critics approach CWM in such a shrill tone? Even if their arguments were somewhat better, would it not be more appropriate for them to gently urge the young songwriters to move in better directions, rather than to dismiss the entire movement as worthless? One suspects that the critics' problems with CWM are not merely theological, but personal, even emotional. It seems that they *just don't like* CWM, and they are searching for reasons (however inadequate those reasons may be to an objective reader) to justify that dislike.

I believe that there are two factors underlying this visceral dislike of CWM. The first is tradition: Writers of the theological establishment don't like CWM because it is nontraditional. Or to put it in more emotional terms, CWM is not what they are used to. The second factor is a feeling that CWM is not "good" music, which I discussed in chapter 10. Here let us focus on tradition.

Marva Dawn presents her position as an attempt to balance tradition and reformation.[1] "Tradition," she says, "along with its correlative authority, was one of the strongest sinews that held western society together."[2] She quotes David Wells as saying that "tradition is the process whereby one generation inducts its successor into its accumulated wisdom, lore, and values."[3] Wells then goes on to say that previous conduits of tradition (family, public education) have capitulated to such things as film and television, so that "in the new civilization that is emerging, children are lifted away from the older values like anchorless boats on a rising tide."[4] Dawn also fears that "getting rid of the old traditions, of course, also means getting rid of denominational loyalties."[5] She emphasizes the importance of maintaining tradition, without "becoming completely alien to the culture."[6] In the interest of balance, she says,

> To accent either pole of this dialectic without the other is to lose them both. To utilize only new worship forms without connections to the past heritage is to isolate only a few years out of the 3,500-year history of the Judeo-Christian tradition. Reformation always returns to and deepens the gifts of the original. On the other hand, without reformation the tradition becomes distorted, stale, or dead—or an idolatry.
>
> Throughout this book, therefore, we will try to balance the two poles of tradition and revitalization, old and new. We will preserve the tradition of faith without letting it become ossified and inaccessible. Simultaneously, we want to participate in the present culture without thereby losing our soul.[7]

As I show in my review of Dawn's book *Reaching Out Without Dumbing Down* (appendix 1), however, it contains few, if any, suggestions for reformation in worship—only warnings against certain ways of seeking reform. Except for theoretical affirmations of the need for balance, Dawn's book is in fact rather unbalanced.

D. G. Hart seems even less interested in reformation.

> What evangelicals who prefer P&W to older liturgies share with academics who teach Louis L'Amour instead of Shakespeare is an inability to see the value of restraint, habit, and form. Evangelicals and the academic left believe that we need to be liberated from the past, from formalism, and from existing structures in order to come into a more intimate relationship with life or the divine. This is really quite astounding in the case of evangelicals whose public reputation depends on defending traditional morality. Yet, the effort to remove all barriers to the expression and experience of the individual self is unmistakably present in the efforts to make worship more expressive and spontaneous. This impulse in evangelical worship repudiates the wisdom of various Christian traditions that, rather than trying to liberate the self in order to experience greater intimacy with God, hold that individuals, because of a tendency to sin and commit idolatry, need to conform to revealed and ordered patterns of faith and practice. The traditions that Presbyterians follow, for instance, are not done to throttle religious experience but rather, as the prescribed means of communing with God and his people. . . . Presbyterians have conducted public and family worship in specific ways because they believe that worship should conform to God's revealed truth. But just as the academic left has abandoned the great works of Western civilization because of a desire for relevance in higher education, so evangelicals have rejected the various elements and forms that have historically informed Protestant worship, again, because they are boring to today's youth.[8]

Hart here virtually identifies the traditional forms of worship with the Word of God. We must worship in traditional ways, he says, because God has commanded us to. It is only by using the traditional forms that worship can "conform to God's revealed truth."

Scripture and Tradition

My perspective, as you might guess, is rather different. First of all, it is important for us to clear up confusion on the relation between church tradition and God's prescriptions. As I indicated in chapter 2 and elsewhere, worship should observe the *sola Scriptura* principle, the doctrine that everything we do in worship must be done in obedience to a command of God. In Presbyterian tradition (!), this is called the "regulative principle of worship."

The Protestant Reformers used *sola Scriptura* as a new broom to sweep clean many of the traditions of the Roman church. They did not abandon tradition entirely. Indeed, their very allegiance to Scripture was a loyalty to the most fundamental Christian tradition, the tradition from which all other tradition springs. And many of the liturgical changes instituted by the Reformers were based on practices going back to the first four centuries of the church. The Reformers knew the writings of the church fathers well, and they appreciated many of the traditions described in the fathers' writings.

But they were also critics of church tradition. They argued that synods and councils not only can err, but have erred. For them, conciliar documents and the writings of past theologians must be tested by the criterion of Scripture and must be abandoned if found unscriptural.

Although the Reformers appreciated tradition, they never identified church traditions with "God's revealed truth." It is certainly true, as Hart says, that Presbyterians have worshiped the way they do because they were trying to make worship conform to God's revelation. But Lutherans, Anglicans, Baptists, and charismatics have also sought to worship scripturally. All of these traditions must be tested by the Bible.

Further, these traditions are not merely repetitions of the precepts of Scripture. Rather, they attempt to *apply* Scripture to various questions about which Scripture does not speak explicitly. Scripture does not tell us whether to use hymnals or overhead transparencies. The use of hymnals is a tradition, one that may or may not be worth continuing. Are we compelled to use hymnals in order to conform to God's truth? The equation of tradition with divine truth is more persuasive in the abstract than in concrete examples like hymnals and overhead projectors! Certainly we should not suggest that we must keep all traditions in order to conform to God's truth. That vastly oversimplifies the issues to be resolved.

As I have argued, it is important to follow Scripture, and it is also important to communicate Scripture to our time. Hart doesn't even raise the issue of communication. Evidently he thinks that is not a problem: we can communicate perfectly well by doing everything as it has been done for hundreds of years. I believe this position does not stand up to even the slightest scrutiny.

It seems to me that the critics of CWM, including Wells, Dawn, Mark Beach, Cornelius Plantinga, and Hart, need to be reminded of *sola Scriptura*. I pointed out earlier that Wells and Dawn base their major arguments on history and sociology rather than biblical theology. The same is clearly true of Hart. The present point is that *sola Scriptura* requires us to have some measure of critical perspective on tradition.

This point ought to be obvious to Protestants. Even Roman Catholics, who rarely recognize any deficiencies in tradition, need to make choices between those traditions which are inconsistent with one another. For Protestants, the question is not whether we should be critical of tradition, but rather how that criticism should be carried out. To claim as Hart seems to that any abandonment of tradition must be based on a postmodern ideology is nonsense.

Traditionalism and Theological Method

I find here again, as in earlier chapters of this book, that there are real problems of theological method underlying the debates about worship. There exists among the critics of CWM—sometimes more blatantly, sometimes more subtly—an equation of Scripture and tradition, of dogmatic and historical theology. In a recent presbytery debate on these issues, a fellow presbyter attacked my view of worship by telling me that I had not sufficiently "interacted" with the Presbyterian tradition: Gillespie, Owen, Bannerman, Girardeau, and the like. He was not willing to engage my scriptural arguments unless I would first refute all the exegetical work of these traditional thinkers. Being a systematic theologian and apologist, rather than a historian of doctrine, it seemed to me that this was an unreasonable request. Similarly, T. David Gordon, responding to an earlier article of mine on the regulative principle of worship, says that these matters will have to be discussed only in a "history of doctrine framework."[9]

In my mind, this confusion is related to the recent tendency of evangelical writers to substitute historical and sociological research for exegesis. In appendix 2, I note this tendency in several writers, including David Wells, with some surprise, since Wells's whole point is that our thinking be governed by theology rather than by secular thought. Dawn's book also tries to put everything into a scriptural-theological framework, but it too is heavy on the sociological and experiential data. Early in the book, Dawn says, "This book's content has been gathered not only from sociological data but also from experiences in specific churches, though their identities are purposely hidden."[10] Her omission of Scripture as a primary source of the book's content may be accidental or simply beyond the context of the sentence. But the sentence does, unfortunately, describe the main emphasis of her book. Like Wells's volumes, Dawn's is experientially rich, theologically thin.

The Place of Tradition According to Scripture

It is actually rather difficult to find in Scripture itself an affirmation of tradition. Scripture uses the term "tradition" mostly in negative senses, as in Matthew 15:6 (cf. Mark 7:4, 8, with background in Isa. 29:13). In that passage, Jesus rebukes the Pharisees, saying, "You nullify the word of God for the sake of your tradition." As we saw in our discussion of *sola Scriptura,* Scripture gives to God's Word alone ultimate authority over human affairs and warns us never to add to that Word or subtract from it. Of course that Word must be applied to situations, and that requires human wisdom. The accumulation of such wisdom over the years constitutes tradition. That tradition is not necessarily bad; but it may not compete with God's Word as a standard for faith and life. (Compare Col. 2:6; 1 Peter 1:18.)

There are a few passages in which "tradition" is used in a favorable sense. In 2 Thessalonians 2:15 and 3:6, it refers to the teaching of the apostles, which they "passed down" to the churches. In these passages, therefore, the tradition is the Word of God itself, not human reflection on or application of the Word.

So it is hard to find in Scripture itself exhortations to worship according to the traditions of the church above and beyond the teachings of the Word of God. Scripture is more concerned to rebuke those who place human traditions on too high a level of authority. Nevertheless, as I indicated, it does not follow that tradition is wrong in itself. Indeed, human thinking, hence tradition, is necessary, if the Word of God is to be applied to present situations. And it must be so applied if it is to function as God intended.

The New Testament does warrant the offices of elder and deacon in the churches, and the writer to the Hebrews exhorts us to obey these leaders (13:17) and follow their example (13:7). This submission is not limited to leaders who are presently living and actively ruling the congregation. In Hebrews 13:7, the author urges his readers to "remember" those leaders whom God gave to the church in the past, those whom God used to found the church. It follows that we should respect not only our present teachers, but those whom God has given to the church in past centuries. In other words, God wants us to respect the traditions of doctrine and life that have developed over the history of the church. That does not mean that traditions are infallible. It does mean that they should be heard with respect.

The above paragraph represents the best argument I know to show that Scripture itself warrants respect for the traditions of the church. I consider it a cogent argument, and therefore I do urge respect for tradition. But I cannot help pointing out that in the

Bible there is actually more emphasis on reformation, on critique of tradition, than there is upon respect for tradition. Certainly, then, we should be careful that our respect for the past not get out of hand.

Is CWM Untraditional?

Dawn's position, at least in her theoretical and programmatic statements, is far sounder and more balanced than Hart's. She understands that tradition needs to be revised from time to time. Her main concerns are (1) that tradition not be entirely abandoned, and (2) that reformations be a kind of organic development of tradition, adapting the tradition to new situations. The second point is my interpretation of what she calls the "dialectic" of tradition and reformation. Dawn's comments about how both tradition and reformation need one another are excellent insights.

But how do these insights work out in practice, especially in regard to CWM?

First, let me point out that no advocate of CWM wants to abandon tradition altogether. Certainly I do not want to do that. CWM-oriented writers, to be sure, have said things about how old-fashioned music tends to bore modern people and the like. But to say that is certainly not to abandon the entire liturgical tradition of Christianity.

CWM itself is very traditional in its way. What could be more traditional than praise, or than the use of psalm and other Scripture texts? As I pointed out earlier, there are also CWM versions of the Apostles' Creed and the Lord's Prayer, and of many traditional hymns. There are a great many CWM songs that serve as calls to worship, introductions to the Lord's Supper, preparations for hearing Scripture, responses to God's Word. I also mentioned that in CWM there is actually an *archaizing* tendency—a diction and cadence much more like the Psalms than like the hymnody of the last three hundred years.

When we compare CWM with traditional liturgy, it is important to compare apples with apples. It is something of an apples to oranges comparison when people measure CWM songs against traditional hymns like "A Mighty Fortress" or "O Sacred Head, Now Wounded." In such comparisons, the CWM songs always come out looking short and superficial. But of course music is also used in other ways in the traditional liturgy. Besides the longer hymns, there have been short songs: the Gloria Patri, the Doxology, the Sanctus, the Gloria in Excelsis, the Sursum Corda, and so on, used as introductions and responses. In my view, CWM songs are best understood in the tradition of these short songs. Compare the Gloria Patri:

> Glory be to the Father,
>   and to the Son,
>   and to the Holy Ghost.
> As it was in the beginning,
>   is now, and ever shall be,
>   world without end, Amen, Amen.

to Donna Adkins's "Glorify Your Name":[11]

> Father, we love You, we worship and adore You,
> Glorify Your name in all the earth.
> Glorify Your name, glorify Your name,
> Glorify Your name in all the earth.
> [Verses 2 and 3 substitute "Jesus" and "Spirit" for
>   "Father."]

Some readers may be horrified that I have even dared to make such a comparison! But the two songs are really very similar in content. Both are explicitly Trinitarian. Both offer praise to God in three persons. Both seek the greater glory of God, extended throughout the universe. The main difference between the two is that the Gloria conceives the world in temporal terms (past, present, and future) while "Glorify Your Name" speaks of it in spatial terms ("in all the earth"). Both conceptions are scriptural and are of theological importance.

Both songs are fairly short, though Adkins's song has three stanzas. I think the best use of Adkins's song is like that of the

Gloria. It should occur at a point in the service where the congregation has been forcefully reminded of God's greatness and goodness, when the worshipers need to express simple, short, but powerful praise.

As worship leader at New Life Presbyterian Church of Escondido, I use both traditional and contemporary songs. I use CWM songs mainly as calls to worship, introductions, and responses to various elements in the service. Sometimes I use CWM songs as responses to traditional hymns. It may sound strange to use a song as a response to a song, but why not? The traditional hymns typically contain rich teaching, and the CWM song may be a good way to say "Amen" to the teaching of the traditional hymn. This seems to me to produce an edifying blend of the traditional and contemporary, and it uses contemporary songs in a rather traditional way.

In any case, it is not an abandonment of tradition to include in worship short, simple songs of praise. The tradition has regularly included these. It has also, of course, included short spoken sentences, like

> MINISTER: The Lord be with you.
> CONGREGATION: And with your spirit.

Certainly these sentences do not have any more theological depth than the average CWM song. But liturgical theologians regularly give to such sentences the highest recommendations while relegating CWM songs to the ash heap.[12]

Denominationalism

We noted earlier in passing a remark of Dawn that "Getting rid of the old traditions, of course, also means getting rid of denominational loyalties."[13] In a recent discussion of worship at the General Assembly of my denomination, a fellow minister asked me how, on my view, we can show ourselves to the world as "distinctively Presbyterian."

I believe that opponents of CWM are concerned not only with

CWM's supposed departure from the traditions of the church universal but also with the fact that CWM may represent a tradition other than that of their own denominations. We have seen that CWM does not depart radically from the traditions of the church universal. But does it depart unduly from specific denominational traditions, and should it criticized on that account?

It is certainly true that CWM is neither specifically Lutheran, Presbyterian, Anglican, or Baptist. If anything, it emerged in a background of charismatic theology, though for the most part it does not urge charismatic distinctives upon the worshiper. One might argue that CWM is anti-Presbyterian, or anti-Lutheran, or whatever, simply because it doesn't stress the distinctives of those traditions. But that would certainly be unfair. Those traditions also share many traditional hymns that do not emphasize their own distinctives. Presbyterians love to sing Luther's "A Mighty Fortress," and Lutherans usually don't complain about Reginald Heber's "Holy, Holy, Holy." Each denomination has some hymns that stress its distinctive positions, but each also uses many hymns that do not.

CWM certainly does represent a different style of music than has been traditional in most confessional denominations. We have discussed style in previous chapters. From that discussion I conclude that we should not treasure our denominational liturgical styles so highly as to make them immune to reformation.

I do suspect that among the critics of CWM there is a scripturally unacceptable kind of denominational pride. In my earlier book *Evangelical Reunion*,[14] I argued that denominations themselves are not warranted by Scripture and that they are due to sin: either sin on the part of those who leave one denomination to start another, or on the part of those in the original body who force people to leave on account of conscience. Although I do not argue that we must instantly reunite all the denominations, I do believe that we should work toward that goal. One means of working toward that goal is to recognize honestly the imperfections of our own denominations and the genuine blessings of God upon denominations other than our own. Another means is to soften the traditional rhetoric and look beneath the matters of interdenominational controversy in order to see what the Word of God actually says about them. Again, we must get away from a traditionalist theological method and back to *sola Scriptura*.

Although I am a Presbyterian, I confess that I do not share my fellow minister's desire for us always to "look like Presbyterians" before the watching world. Certainly I believe that we should present to the world the insights of biblical Presbyterianism: divine sovereignty, plural eldership, and so on. But it is not my goal to get people to say, "Oh, you're a Presbyterian!" I am far happier when people hear my arguments and say, "Oh, you're teaching what the Bible says."

Denominational pride does turn off seekers today. And to a great extent they are right to be turned off by it. God does not delight in the fact that his church is divided into thousands of different groups, all in competition with one another. Denominational division is a tragedy, a shame for the church. We cannot eliminate those divisions overnight. Certainly it will not help to abandon our denominational connections and make our congregations independent. After all, an independent church is a denomination with one congregation.

But we should try to reduce as much as possible the significance of denominationalism. Rather than parading it pridefully, as if our identity were rooted mainly in our differences with others, we should give due emphasis to and seek to build on what we truly hold in common. We should take up every opportunity to work together with Christians of other denominational traditions, to achieve better mutual understanding, broader agreements, greater love, and, eventually, the abolition of the divisions themselves. One major task for denominations in our time is to pray and work themselves out of existence.

CWM is potentially a major ecumenical force. It does unite believers of many denominations and traditions. It focuses on common, core beliefs, rather than on what divides. Along with that, there is certainly an important place for hymns that emphasize denominational distinctives. If we believe those distinctives to be scriptural, we ought to sing about them. But we should also make glad use of hymns that unite us to Christians outside our immediate circle. Many traditional hymns help us to do that, and CWM songs provide additional help in that direction. In my mind, that is a virtue, not a fault, in the CWM genre.

Tradition and Reformation

Have I maintained Dawn's "dialectic" of tradition and reformation? Recall her appeal for balance:

> To accent either pole of this dialectic without the other is to lose them both. To utilize only new worship forms without connections to the past heritage is to isolate only a few years out of the 3,500-year history of the Judeo-Christian tradition. Reformation always returns to and deepens the gifts of the original. On the other hand, without reformation the tradition becomes distorted, stale, or dead— or an idolatry.[15]

Though I am not willing to put as much value on tradition as do Dawn and Hart, my suggested uses of CWM make significant connections to the past. I have suggested using CWM songs in ways that the church has traditionally used hymns, particularly short hymns of praise. I have also recommended that we continue to use traditional hymnody, taking advantage of its theological depth.

Dawn may not agree with my application of her dialectical principle. The principle itself is rather vague. There is no form of worship in the church today that doesn't have significant connections to the past. Almost anything done today could arguably serve in part to "return to and deepen the gifts of the original," even when accompanied by anti-traditional rhetoric. Most of Dawn's additional guidance on how to carry out this principle is also rather vague, so it is hard to say what fulfills it and what does not. Of course, the principle is fine in itself, and it does challenge us to greater efforts to achieve a truly integral relation between old and new.

In any case, I am not asking the church to do anything different from what it has always done: praise, prayer, Word, sacrament, and so on. I ask only that we do these things in ways that communicate adequately to people today, in accordance with the Pauline emphasis on intelligibility in 1 Corinthians 14. The Protestant churches have always been willing to speak the languages of the worshipers, so the importance of contextualization in music as well as word should need no argument. Contextualization in this sense is very traditional. Therefore I think CWM can be a helpful tool for us as we seek to communicate God's Word in God's way.

Dealing with Our Emotions

I realize, however, that much of what I have been saying may fall on deaf ears because the traditionalist opposition to CWM is, in my judgment, not wholly based on theology. There is a large emotional component to it. I know of no other way to explain the shoddy argumentation and the sheer stubbornness of the CWM critics. They often seem locked in cement on this issue, even when the rational considerations obviously support the other side. It is rather ironic that the traditionalist position has such a large emotional component to it. As we have seen, liturgical traditionalists, particularly in Reformed circles, tend to be intellectualist and anti-emotionalist in their concept of what takes place in worship. But in any case we must address the emotional issue.

We should face the fact that liturgical change is never easy, especially for mature Christians who have been worshiping for a long time. It is not easy to lose the songs you have grown up with and to be forced into a whole new language of worship. The old songs are one's native language of worship. We know that immigrants to the United States who learn English and use it most of the time, nevertheless often prefer to use their original language when they pray silently or audibly. Similarly, one's musical language of worship does not change easily.

As I mentioned earlier, I am a classical musician by training and preference. After worshiping for most of forty years in highly traditional Presbyterian churches, I moved to Escondido, California, and found myself as director of worship in the recently planted New

Life Presbyterian Church. There I was dragged kicking and scream-
ing into the world of CWM. At first I feared that I would never
again be allowed to sing "When Morning Gilds the Skies" or
"Crown Him with Many Crowns." But that anxiety soon passed,
as old and young among us bent to meet one another's needs. We
kept many (not all) of the old songs and added a lot of CWM songs.
Some of the latter I liked immediately; some I liked after many hearings; still others I never liked very much. But we persevered and
over the last sixteen years developed a style of worship with which
I and the congregation have become fairly comfortable.

God's grace enabled me to persevere through the discomfort.
The main biblical considerations motivating me through this time
were the Great Commission and the emphasis on intelligible worship in 1 Corinthians 14. We wanted to have a form of worship
that spoke intelligibly to the community we sought to reach: not
only long-time Presbyterians, but also non-Presbyterian Christians
and the unchurched. To reach that goal, we all needed to put
aside, to a large extent, our own prejudices and preferences, to
esteem the interests of others above our own. God blessed that
desire, and many came to a saving knowledge of Christ through
the church's ministry.

That is my response to the emotional problems of those facing
the loss, or partial loss, of tradition: God wants us to count all
things but loss for the sake of Christ. That works both ways, of
course. Both those who love traditional hymns and those who love
the new songs need to be flexible, to understand one another and
minister to one another. What we must not do is to lash out at
one another with false pretensions to knowledge, sophistication,
and rationality, and with intellectual arguments that are little more
than masks for underlying anger.

Notes

1. Marva Dawn, *Reaching Out Without Dumbing Down* (Grand Rapids:
Eerdmans, 1995), 58–60.

2. Ibid., 58.

3. Ibid. She quotes David Wells, *No Place for Truth* (Grand Rapids: Eerdmans, 1993), 84.

4. Dawn, *Reaching Out,* 58.

5. Ibid., 144.

6. Ibid., 59.

7. Ibid., 60. Cf. 144–48.

8. D. G. Hart, "Post-modern Evangelical Worship," *Calvin Theological Journal* 30 (1995), 456.

9. T. David Gordon, "Some Answers About the Regulative Principle," *Westminster Theological Journal* 55 (fall 1993), 329. In context, Gordon is complaining about what he considers to be my caricature of the Reformed "traditional" view of worship. However, he does not disagree with my description of that tradition in any of the specifics relevant to my critique.

10. Dawn, *Reaching Out,* 11.

11. MMPCB, 123. I have taken the liberty of substituting "Your" for "Thy" before "name." The version in MMPCB has "You" in the first line, then "Thy name" thereafter. I think the pronouns should be made consistent in one direction or the other.

12. For an example, note Dawn's lavish praise for these short worship sentences, discussed in appendix 1. She appears to be unaware that the same value can be found in CWM choruses.

13. Dawn, *Reaching Out,* 144.

14. Grand Rapids: Baker, 1991. The book is no longer in print.

15. Dawn, *Reaching Out,* 60.

CHAPTER 12

❧

My CWM Song Book

Some readers may be persuaded that it is appropriate to use CWM songs in worship, but they do not know where to begin. The CWM literature is extensive. The best way to get started, of course, is to get advice from somebody who knows CWM and who agrees with you on criteria of quality. I have indicated through this book what my criteria are. As the director of worship in New Life Presbyterian Church (PCA) in Escondido, California, I look for songs that are consistent with Scripture and Reformed doctrine, excellent in musical and poetic quality, and singable—songs that communicate well with people today. Some readers, therefore, may be interested to know specifically what songs we use at New Life.

So I conclude this book with a list of songs. This list does not contain all the songs that we use in worship. Many CWM songs are passed around informally, one person learning from another, or learning from a tape. So we sing some songs that have never been published and/or whose authorship has been forgotten. I will not include those on this list, even though they are among our favorites. I couldn't begin to tell you how to find them. I will include on this list only songs for which I can list a publisher or at least an author. (For an annual fee, churches can obtain rights to use many of these songs through the CCLI program. Contact Christian Copyright Licensing, Inc., 17201 N.E. Sacramento St., Portland, OR 97203.)

Many of these songs we sing differently from the published versions: more elaborate accompaniments, rhythmic, harmonic, and melodic changes. In some cases, those changes make the difference between an average and an outstanding song. But I will not seek to explain all these variations. I will claim only that the following songs have the potential to be useful in the worship of God.

I do not pretend that this list is up-to-date, or that it contains all and only the best of CWM. I am probably ignorant of much that is recent and good. This list is nothing more or less than the list of hymns I have taught to my congregation over the last seventeen years, together with some that I plan to teach in the future.

I should remind the reader that we also use a great many traditional hymns, as well as contemporary pieces that are not classifiable as CWM. We have not found the combination of styles to be unwieldy. Some may be interested to know that in 1987, Maranatha! Music published a volume called *100 Hymns, 100 Choruses,* which includes songs of both genres. In the back, there are suggestions for medleys including both, such as

> "Come, We That Love the Lord"
> "He Has Made Me Glad"
> "Glorious Things of Thee Are Spoken"
> "Therefore the Redeemed"

I have not made much use of this book, but it is good to be aware that in this case Maranatha!, the fountainhead of CWM, recommended combinations of genres. Such medleys also appear often in CWM records.

Sources will be abbreviated as follows:

ALMC   *Abundant Life Music Company: Church Life Collection* (Santa Clarita, Calif.: Abundant Life Music

Company, 1997). Write Abundant Life Music Company at P.O. Box 802515, Santa Clarita, CA 91380-2515. Phone 800-870-7162.

GP1–3   *Glory and Praise* (Phoenix: North American Liturgy Resources, 1977). These volumes were produced by Roman Catholics for use in their worship. Although I am firmly Protestant, I find many of these songs useful.

MMPCB   *Maranatha! Music Praise Chorus Book* (Laguna Hills, Calif.: Maranatha! Music, 1993). Other editions as noted.

MMPWC   *Maranatha! Music Praise and Worship Collection* (No place of publication listed: Maranatha! Music, 1987).

SS1   *Scripture in Song.* Vol. 1 (Nashville: Benson, 1979).

SS2   *Scripture in Song.* Vol. 2 (Nashville: Benson, 1981).

TH   *Trinity Hymnal* (Philadelphia: Great Commission, 1991).

WCISG   *Why Can't I See God?* By Judy Rogers (no publication date). Write Judy Rogers, P.O. Box 888442, Atlanta, GA 30338. These songs were written with children in mind, but I consider many of them excellent for congregational worship.

WH   *Worship Him* (Alexandria, Ind.: Tempo Music, distributed by Alexandria House, 1983).

WSV   *Worship Songs of the Vineyard* (Franklin, Tenn.: Mercy/Vineyard). This a series of seven volumes so far; I expect to see additional volumes published.

"All Heaven Declares" (the Glory of the Risen Lord), by Noel and Tricia Richards. MMPCB, 4.

"All I Have" (James 1:16–18), by Cheryl Marshall. ALMC, 33.

"All the Ends of the Earth" (Ps. 98), by Bob Dufford. GP3, 174.

"Alleluia," by Jerry Sinclair. MMPCB, 169.

"Amazing Love," by Graham Kendrick. Integrity Music, P.O. Box 851622, Mobile, AL 36685-1622.

"As the Deer" (Ps. 42:1), by Martin Nystrom. MMPCB, 28.

"As We Gather," by Mike Fay and Tom Coomes. MMPCB, 16.

"Awesome God," by Rich Mullins. MMPCB, 161.

"Awesome in Power," by Rick Founds. MMPCB, 104.

"The Battle Belongs to the Lord," by Jamie Owens-Collins. MMPCB, 268.

"Be Exalted, O God" (Pss. 57:9–11; 97:9; 108:3–5), by Brent Chambers. MMPCB, 25.

"Behold, What Manner of Love" (1 John 3:1), by Patricia Van Tine. MMPCB, 45.

"Beloved, Let Us Love One Another" (1 John 4:7–8), by Dennis Ryder. MMPCB, 62.

"Blessed Be the Lord God" (Ps. 72:18–19), by Shirley Powell. SS1, 18.

"Blessed Be the Lord God Almighty," by Bob Fitts. MMPCB, 6.

"Blest Be the Lord" (Ps. 91), by Dan Schutte, GP1, 10.

"A Broken and a Humble Heart" (Ps. 51:17), by Cheryl Marshall. ALMC, 23.

"Cares Chorus" (1 Peter 5:7), by Kelly Willard. MMPCB, 48.

"The Child of Bethlehem," by Dan Burgess. MMPCB, 294.

"Clap, Clap Your Hands," by Jennifer Randolph. Integrity Music, P.O. Box 851622, Mobile, AL 36685-1622.

"Clap Your Hands" (Ps. 47:1), by Jimmy Owens. WH, 154.

"Clean Hands and a Pure Heart" (Ps. 24:3–5, 2 Chron. 16:9), by Dale Garratt. SS2, 230.

"Come and See," by Lenny LeBlanc. MMPCB, 131.

"Come and Sing Praises" (Ascribe to the Lord), by Morris Chapman and Greg Massanari. MMPCB, 58.

"Come into His Presence," by Lynn Baird. Integrity Music, P.O. Box 851622, Mobile, AL 36685-1622.

"Come into the Holy of Holies," by John Sellers. MMPCB, 71.

"Come, Let Us Worship and Bow Down" (Ps. 95:6–7), by Dave Doherty. MMPCB, 105.

"Create in Me," by Mary Rice Hopkins. MMPCB, 74.

"Cry of My Heart," by Terry Butler. MMPCB, 164.

"The Easter Song," by Annie Herring. Latter Rain Music.

"Father, I Adore You," by Terrye Coelho. MMPCB, 151.

"Fortress of Love" (Ps. 18:2), by Cheryl Marshall. ALMC, 23.

"Freely, Freely," by Carol Owens. MMPCB, 1st ed., 18.

"Give Ear to My Words" (Ps. 5:1–3), by Bill Sprouse, Jr. MMPCB, 220.

"Give Thanks," by Henry Smith. MMPCB, 7.

"Glorify Thy Name" (Ps. 86:12), by Donna Adkins. MMPCB, 123.

"Glorify You," by Lenny LeBlanc. MMPCB, 129.

"Glory, Glory Hallelujah," by James Ward. Write him at New City Fellowship Music Department, 2424 E. Third St., Chattanooga, TN 37404; or contact Music Anno Domini, Box 7465, Grand Rapids, MI 49510.

"God Can Do Anything," by Judy Rogers. WCISG, 18.

"God Is a Spirit" (John 4:24) by Judy Rogers. WCISG, 13.

"God Made Me," by Judy Rogers. WCISG, 4.

"Great and Marvelous!" (Rev. 15:3–4), by George C. Miladin. Write Rev. George Miladin, 2555 Evergreen St., San Diego, CA 92106.

"Great Is the Lord," by Michael W. Smith and Deborah D. Smith. MMPCB, 11.

"He Has Made Me Glad" (Pss. 100:4; 118:24), by Leona Von Brethorst. MMPCB, 18.

"He Has Shown Thee" (Mic. 6:8), by Bob Sklar. MMPCB, 250.

"He Is Exalted," by Twila Paris. MMPCB, 111.

"He Is Holy," by Walt Harrah and John Schreiner. MMPCB, 56.

"He Is Lord" (Phil. 2:10–11), composer unknown. MMPCB, 126.

"Hear My Cry" (Ps. 61:1, 2), composer unknown. MMPCB, 2d ed., 215.

"The Heavens Are Telling" (Ps. 19:1, 7), by Andrew J. Noch. Write him at 5419 La Cuenta Dr., San Diego, CA 92124-1416.

"Heroes of Faith" (Heb. 11) by Jamie Turner and Joan Pinkston (Greenville, S.C.: Bob Jones University Press, 1988).

"His Name Is Wonderful," by Audrey Mieir. MMPCB, 108.

"Holy Father" (Ps. 95:2), by Cheryl Marshall. ALMC, 6.

"Holy, Holy, Holy Is the Lord of Hosts" (Isa. 6:3), by Nolene Prince. MMPCB, 152.

"Hosanna," by Carl Tuttle. MMPCB, 163.

"How Lovely Are Thy Dwelling Places" (Ps. 84:1–3), by Bin Soto. SS1, 171.

"How Majestic Is Your Name" (uses Ps. 8:1), by Michael W. Smith. MMPCB, 217.

"Humble Thyself in the Sight of the Lord" (1 Peter 5:5–6; James 4:10), by Bob Hudson. MMPCB, 166.

"I Am Convinced" (Rom. 8:38–39), by Kitty Stanton. Write her at 755 Butterfield Lane, San Marcos, CA 92069.

"I Can Do All Things" (Phil. 4:13), by Cheryl Marshall. ALMC, 26.

"I Love You, Lord," by Laurie Klein. MMPCB, 21.

"I Need You," by Rick Founds. MMPCB, 109.

"I Will Call upon the Lord," by Michael O'Shields (2 Sam. 22:4, 47). MMPCB, 180.

"I Will Celebrate," by Linda Duvall. MMPCB, 112.

"I Will Sing of the Mercies" (Ps. 89:1), by J. H. Fillmore. MMPCB, 66.

"I Will Sing Unto the Lord" (Ex. 15:1–2) (The Horse and the Rider), author unknown. SS1, 168.

"I Will Trust in You," by Danny Daniels. MMPCB, 315.

"If My People Will Pray" (2 Chron. 7:14), by Jimmy Owens. Bud John Songs, Inc.

"I'll Never Be Forsaken" (Heb. 13:5), by Cheryl Marshall. ALMC, 27.

"Immanuel," by Andy Park. WSV3, 78.

"In God the Father I Believe" (The Apostles' Creed) by George Miladin (see John 21:15–17). Write Rev. George Miladin, 2555 Evergreen St., San Diego, CA 92106.

"Ineffable Exchange," by Jacques LeFevre and George Miladin. Write Rev. George Miladin, 2555 Evergreen St., San Diego, CA 92106.

"It Is Good to Give Thanks" (Ps. 92:1–2), by Tom Howard and Bill Batstone. MMPCB, 273.

"Jesus, Draw Me Close," by Rick Founds. MMPCB, 73.

"Jesus, Name Above All Names," by Nadia Hearn. MMPCB 47.

"Jesus, You Are Lord," by Rick Founds. MMPCB, 165.

"Job's Song," by Andrew John Noch. Write him at 5419 La Cuenta Dr., San Diego, CA 92124-1416.

"Keep Looking Up" (Heb. 12:2), by James Ward. Write him at New City Fellowship Music Department, 2424 E. Third St., Chattanooga, TN 37404; or contact Anno Domini Music, P.O. Box 7465, Grand Rapids, MI 49510.

"King of Kings" (Rev. 19:16), by Sophie Conty and Naomi Batya. MMPCB, 137.

"Lamb of God," by Twila Paris. MMPCB, 2d ed., 7.

"The Law of the Lord" (Ps. 19:7–11), author unknown. MMPCB, 1st ed., 1983, 118.

"Let All That Is Within Me," by Melvin Harrel. WH, 41.

"Let All the Earth" (Shout for Joy), by Rick Founds. MMPCB, 2d ed., 64.

"Let Us Exalt His Name Together" (Ps. 34), by Stuart Dauermann.

"Lift Up Your Heads," by Steven Fry. SS2, 13.

"Lord, Be Glorified," by Bob Kilpatrick. MMPCB, 176.

"Lord, I Lift Your Name on High," by Rick Founds. MMPCB, 199.

"The Lord Is My Light" (Ps. 27:1), by Walt Harrah. MMPCB, 64.

"Lord of Glory," by Tim Manion. GP1, 37.

"The Lord Reigns" (Ps. 97:1, 3, 5), by John Sellers. MMPCB, 127.

"Majesty," by Jack Hayford. MMPCB, 212.

"Make a Noise" (Ps. 100), by Terry Clark. Clark Brothers Communications.

"Make Me a Servant," by Kelly Willard. MMPCB, 236.

"Make Your Presence Known," by John Barbour. MMPCB, 49.

"May Your Kingdom Come" (Matt. 6:10), by Kirk Dearman. MMPCB, 34.

"Meekness and Majesty," by Graham Kendrick. MMPCB, 214.

"Meet Us Here," by Dan Marks. MMPCB, 138.

"More Love, More Power," by Jude Del Hierro. WSV1, 84.

"No Bad News" (Ps. 112), by James Ward. Write him at New City Fellowship Music Department, 2424 E. Third St., Chattanooga, TN 37404; or contact Anno Domini Music, P.O. Box 7465, Grand Rapids, MI 49510.

"O Lord, You're Beautiful," by Keith Green. MMPCB, 310.

"O Magnify the Lord," by Michael O'Shields. MMPWC, 4.

"Oh How He Loves You and Me," by Kurt Kaiser. MMPCB, 238.

"One Thing Have I Desired" (Ps. 27:4), by Stuart Scott. MMPWC, 31.

"Our God Reigns" (Isa. 52:7–53:12), by Leonard E. Smith, Jr. MMPCB, 219.

"Our God Was, Our God Is" (Job 37:5–13), by Cheryl Marshall. ALMC, 5.

"Peter, Do You Love Me?" (John 21:15–17), by George Miladin to a tune by Thad Jones. Write Rev. George Miladin, 2555 Evergreen St., San Diego, CA 92106.

"Praise the Name of Jesus," by Roy Hicks, Jr. MMPCB, 200.

"Praise Ye the Lord" (Ps. 150), by Lydia F. Stephens. Publication data not available.

"Protector of My Soul," by Anne Barbour. MMPCB, 38.

"Purify My Heart," by Jeff Nelson. MMPCB, 72.

"Rejoice in the Lord Always" (Phil. 4:4), by Evelyn Turner. MMPCB, 239.

"Rising Like a Morning Sun," by James Ward. Write him at New City Fellowship Music Department, 2424 E. Third St., Chattanooga, TN 37404; or contact Music Anno Domini, Box 7465, Grand Rapids, MI 49510.

"Rock of Ages," traditional hymn with new tune by James Ward. TH, 500.

"Rock of My Salvation," by Teresa Muller. MMPCB, 213.

"The Salvation Song," by Judy Rogers. WCISG, 36.

"Seek First the Kingdom" (Matt. 6:25–33), by James Ward. Write him at New City Fellowship Music Department, 2424 E. Third St., Chattanooga, TN 37404; or contact Music Anno Domini, Box 7465, Grand Rapids, MI 49510.

"Seek Ye First" (Matt. 6:33; 4:4; 7:7), by Karen Lafferty. MMPCB, 243.

"A Shield About Me" (Ps. 3:3 [28:7]), by Donn Thomas and Charles Williams. MMPCB, 23.

"Shine, Jesus, Shine," by Graham Kendrick. MMPCB, 2.

"Sing a New Song to the Lord" (Ps. 98), by David G. Wilson and Timothy Dudley-Smith. Hope Publishing.

"Sing Hallelujah," by Linda Stassen. MMPCB, 319.

"Spirit of the Living God," by Daniel Iverson. MMPCB, 277.

"Stand in the Congregation," by Bill Batstone. MMPCB, 313.

"The Steadfast Love of the Lord" (Lam. 3:22–23), by Edith Mc-Neill. MMPCB, 306.

"Strength of My Life," by Leslie Phillips. MMPCB, 288.

"Surely Goodness and Mercy" (Ps. 23:6), by John W. Peterson. SS1, 46.

"The Ten Commandments Song," by Judy Rogers. WCISG, 44.

"There Is a Redeemer," by Melody Green. MMPCB, 244.

"Therefore the Redeemed" (Isa. 35:10; 51:11), by Ruth Lake. MMPCB, 230.

"Therefore with Joy" (Isa. 12:3–4), composer unknown. SS1, 11.

"This Is My Commandment" (John 15:12), composer unknown. MMPCB, 241.

"This Is the Day" (Ps. 118:24), by Les Garrett. MMPCB, 210.

"Thou Art Worthy" (Rev. 5:9), by Pauline Michael Mills. MMPCB, 208.

"Thy Loving Kindness" (Ps. 63:3–4), by Hugh Mitchell. MMPCB, 232.

"Thy Word," by Amy Grant and Michael W. Smith. MMPCB, 234.

"The Trees of the Field" (Isa. 55:12), by Stuart Dauermann and Steffi Karen Rubin. MMPCB, 103.

"Turn Your Eyes Upon Jesus," by Helen Lemmel. MMPCB, 227.

"Unto Thee, O Lord" (Ps. 25), by Charles Monroe. MMPCB, 207.

"We Are Family," by Jimmy and Carol Owens. WH, 141.

"We Believe," by Rick Founds. MMPCB, 231.

"We Bow Down," by Twila Paris. MMPCB, 97.

"We Choose the Fear of the Lord," by Kirk Dearman, MMPCB, 221.

"We Have Come into This House," by Bruce Ballinger. MMPCB, 204.

"When I Look into Your Holiness" (Ps. 34:5), by Wayne and Cathy Perrin. MMPCB, 206.

"Where Could I Go from Your Spirit?" (Ps. 139:7–14) by Kelly Willard. MMPCB, 1st ed., 139.

"White as Snow," by Leon Olguin. MMPCB, 190.

"Who Is Like Unto Thee?" (Ex. 15:11), by Judy Horner. SS1, 167.

"Why Can't I See God?" by Judy Rogers. WCISG, 1.

"You Are Crowned with Many Crowns," by John Sellers. MMPCB, 203.

"You Are My Hiding Place" (Ps. 32:7), by Michael Ledner. MMPCB, 205.

"You Are My Refuge," by Lenny LeBlanc and Greg Gulley. MMPCB, 323.

"You Have Broken the Chains," by Jamie Owens-Collins. Fairhill Music.

APPENDIX 1

❧

Review of Marva Dawn, Reaching Out Without Dumbing Down[1]

When I began to defend the use of Contemporary Worship Music (CWM), friends were quick to suggest things on the other side for me to read. I have referred to a number of these in the text of this book. The most thorough, however, was the book named above. Dawn is a Lutheran lay theologian, widely read in the literature of worship. Her publisher is quite respectable, and reviews of her book are generally favorable. Her approach to the subject is irenic and balanced, yet often forceful. The book shows a generally high quality of thought.

On the subjects of Contemporary Worship (CW) and CWM, however, I do not believe that she succeeds in making her case. Nevertheless, I am happy to have encountered the book, since I have considered her a worthy opponent. She has given me much to think about, and without her assistance in thinking through these issues, the present volume would have been much poorer.

I should mention that Dawn describes her experience of worship during a period when she was undergoing cancer treatment. She does not tell us how those treatments turned out. My prayers continue to be with her, that God will bring complete healing and prevent any recurrence. Because of this situation I am a bit hesitant to criticize the book. But I press on, for Dawn has written a serious book, which she no doubt wants to have scrutinized with care. She often expresses a desire for rational dialogue on these matters which are often so fraught with emotionalism. I hope to provide here some constructive interaction.

The title of the book suggests a major concern with the intellectual quality of worship, but along the way she deals with every subject I have considered in the present volume, and many others besides. We shall begin our consideration of the book where she does, facing the recent decline in the quality of learning in the United States.

Dumbing Down

Early in the book, Dawn notes studies that show steep declines in the intellectual accomplishment of school children in recent years because of "dysfunctional homes, media assaults, lack of creative play time, and many more factors. . . ."[2] Why, she asks, haven't we been more aware of the seriousness of the situation? She answers,

> Part of the reason for our failure to address the crisis is that the problem's immensity has been hidden by schools and agencies "dumbing down" the tests. Healy demonstrates this by showing the astounding difference between a fourth grade reading test from 1964 and one from 1982. She also prints part of an "advanced" reading achievement test for ninth grade from 1988 (pp. 27–36). The "advanced" ninth grade test is shockingly easier than the 1964 fourth grade test![3]

Then she asks concerning the Christian church,

> In what ways do we, too, lack the patience necessary for forming intellect and faith? How has faith formation been disrupted by instant sensory gratification? What resources

does Christian faith provide for renewing and sustaining churches in such a culture and for reaching beyond ourselves to persons of that culture?[4]

"Dumbing down" worship, then, occurs when the church demands too little of its worshipers and thus gives them inadequate intellectual and spiritual nurture.

Rising Above the Worship Wars?

Dawn doesn't quite say that CWM necessarily dumbs down our worship. She tries to rise somewhat above the "worship wars."

Can we find some way to prevent discussions about worship styles from becoming fierce and bitter battles waged between two entrenched camps? Can we instead find common criteria by which to assess what we are doing in worship, so that we can bring together opposing sides of various arguments, so that we can truly be the Church as we talk together about our worship practices?[5]

I applaud these rhetorical questions, and I trust that the present volume represents a contribution to that sort of thoughtful dialogue. The emphasis on "common criteria" is very much to the point.

One would guess from these proposals that Dawn will come out as a moderate, advocating a combination of some CWM with some elements of traditional worship. She does commend some of the concerns that have led some churches to make room for CWM. As we saw in chapter 3, she values freshness in worship, over against tradition that has "grown stale."[6] And she points out that

when we agree that God must be the subject and object of our worship, we discover that the bitter war between "traditional" and "contemporary" styles misses the real issue. Both can easily become idolatrous. . . .

Enthusiasts for contemporary worship are right in seeking to reach out to persons in the culture around us and in rejecting tradition that has grown stale. Those who value the Church's worship heritage are right to question the faithfulness and integrity of many contemporary worship forms and to seek a noticeable difference in worship that underscores the Church's countercultural emphasis. Only in a dialectical tension of tradition and reformation can we ask better questions to insure that worship is consistent with the nature of God as revealed in the Scriptures and in the person of Jesus Christ.[7]

She even says early in the book that

The very fact that congregations so quickly split into opposing sides on so many questions reveals our modern inability to nuance. A computer chip is either on or off, so in this data-bit world we often phrase our arguments in either/or choices. Can we think together along the lines of both/and?[8]

I am not one to rejoice in "dialectical tensions," but I would agree that both tradition and reformation are important in worship. So one might expect that Dawn's book would explore ways of combining the new and the old, ways of achieving "both/and" in our worship.

But that expectation would be disappointed. I may have missed something, but in this 316-page book I did not find one unequivocal commendation of any nontraditional worship practice or of any CWM music. She does sometimes commend "fresh approaches" in very general terms.[9] But rarely does she give any specific examples, and never does she specify CWM or any worship practice that comes out of the CWM milieu. The "common criteria" she suggests uniformly yield conclusions favorable to traditional hymnody and against CWM. When she opposes the new styles, to be sure, she usually speaks tactfully of "many" worship leaders or CWM songs, rather than all; she always leaves to CWM proponents the option of exempting their favorites. But since she never cites any exceptions, the book comes across as being very opposed to the new approaches.

In this book, therefore, there is no credible program of reformation, only a rationale for maintaining tradition and casting suspicion on the new movements. When Dawn commends the effort to "reach out," she evidently believes that can be done adequately through a somewhat creative use of tradition. And when she commends the rejection of "tradition that has grown stale," her solution (I gather, though these are my words, not hers) is not to allow the tradition to grow stale, but to keep it alive through constant creative use. So in practice there is no room in her worship agenda for CWM or anything else that she considers to be nontraditional.

Thus, despite all the sweet reasonableness and the attempt to rise above the battle, the book comes across as a very negative response to contemporary worship styles in general and CWM in particular.

Songs of Substance

As I read the book, I kept wishing that she would take some specific examples of CWM songs and show me how they dumb down worship. She does cite a few examples, such as the ones I noted in chapter 3, but they are either irrelevant to this precise point, or they fail to make her case.

I also hoped she would list systematically the criteria by which she makes her value judgments. Halfway through the book, Dawn does cite Thomas Gieschen, who "proposes a 'selection grid' by which choral directors could screen repertoire choices and discusses how matters of style fit into the selection process."[10] Now at last, I thought, we would get down to business and learn the criteria that actually serve to exclude "much" CWM as too dumb for worship. But again I was disappointed. Most of Gieschen's criteria (and the subcriteria that Dawn attaches to them) are theological, and of course the doctrinal orthodoxy of texts is not an issue between proponents and opponents of CWM.[11] One of

Dawn's subcriteria is dignity of setting,[12] but that too is something different from[13] the issue of intellectual quality, of dumbing down.

The only criterion on the list that seems to me to be relevant to intellectual quality is that we should not use hymns that are "theologically correct but shallow." Dawn quotes Raymond Gawronski in this connection, who describes a modern religious song:

> Written, no doubt, within the past 20 years, it is a piece of that resigned sentimentality that is characteristic of "easy listening music." Although pleasant enough, it is spiritual Wonder Bread: It utterly lacks roots, depth, sustenance. It is all right as a starter, to open the heart to prayer. But unless fed by some solid food . . . serious seekers will turn elsewhere.[14]

But neither Dawn nor Gawronski names the song. Nothing specific, just a string of anti-CWM clichés. The quotation uses various deprecatory metaphors and epithets, but it doesn't take the trouble to show what in the song justifies them.

I don't deny that some CWM songs can be described in these terms. In my book, I have made some similar comments about Bill Gaither's "There's Something About That Name."[15] "Resigned sentimentality" has appeared in many traditions, particularly during the nineteenth century, and no doubt it exists in the CWM literature as well. And there are many songs—again, of many traditions—that we listen to and casually dismiss as lacking substance. I admitted earlier that to me many CWM songs are interchangeable and not particularly memorable.

But let's get down to specifics, if Dawn will not. What about Michael W. Smith's "How Majestic Is Your Name?"[16] Is it resigned sentimentality? Spiritual Wonder Bread? Does it lack roots, depth, sustenance? The first part comes literally from Psalm 8:1, and the rest is Psalms language. Do we want to suggest that God's Word is less than adequately deep, that it furnishes inadequate roots? Does this song have an "easy listening" tune? I think not; in my judgment, the tune has a real bite to it, especially with the accompaniment used on the recorded version.

What about Brent Chambers' "Be Exalted, O God"?[17] Karen Lafferty's "Seek Ye First"?[18] Melody Green's "There Is a Redeemer"?[19] As with many musical traditions, it is much easier to criticize CWM in general than in particular.

Again it seems to me that these most thoughtful critics of CWM don't know the music very well. At crucial points in the argument, they present no specifics, only vague impressions. Therefore, I am not moved from my conviction that a substantial number of CWM songs are indeed worthy to be used in the worship of God.

Worship That Nurtures

In this discussion, we have moved from the intellectual dimension of worship to somewhat broader concerns. That is in keeping with the spirit of Dawn's book, for she wants something more than merely intellectually respectable worship. She wants worship that nurtures, worship that trains people in godliness.

Perhaps the central concern expressed in Dawn's book is that music and worship nurture mature Christian character.

> The Scriptures, the history of the Church, and my own faith, experience, and training convince me that the vitality and faithfulness of our personal and corporate Christian lives and the effectiveness of our outreach in the world around us depend on the character that is formed in us. . . . How can we best reach out to (contemporary) society without "dumbing down" that essential character formation?[20]

Her concern about the influence of modern culture boils down to this one, for she believes that bringing the distinctive elements of modern culture into the church is injurious to the character of God's people. Thus she fears that CWM is counter-productive to Christian character:

> One advocate of "contemporary" music for worship wrote in a nationally published letter to another pastor, "you

mentioned that your contemporary service 'has become your most popular service.' That should surely say something." Shouldn't we look more closely at something that is "popular" to ask if it is being faithful? . . . Is the point of worship to make participants comfortable or to teach them about God? Keeping God as the subject might lead to comfort—or its opposite! What kind of character is being formed by certain styles of worship? Candy is very popular with children, but we wouldn't feed them only candy if we want them to grow up strong and healthy.[21]

So how does the use of CWM injure the character of worshipers? Dawn does not give a clear answer. The later section of the book called "Nurturing Believers' Character" says nothing about CWM and little about any kind of music at all. She says much there about the importance of truth, faithfulness to biblical teaching, honoring God as the main subject of worship, the motivation of the pastor, and so on, with which I have no quarrel. But as I have argued earlier, CWM is God-centered music, and it is mostly scriptural truth in scriptural language. Therefore, one would think that Dawn would commend it as an admirable means of communicating biblical truth to our time and of forming Christian character. But in this context she says nothing that would be helpful in identifying music that builds character.

There is one point in the book where she addresses this issue. She mentions a congregation which "sponsors both a 'traditional' and a 'contemporary' service each Sunday," a split she regards as "destructive to the congregation." On one Sunday, there was a long Scripture reading in both services. The worshipers at the traditional service took the reading in stride. At the contemporary service, however, the pastor

> had to ask if all the readers were there, and before the extended reading he warned the congregation that it was going to be very long and urged them to try to pay attention to its entirety.[22]

She draws morals from the story by asking the following rhetorical questions:

Does our choice of worship music increase or reduce our capacity to listen or to think theologically? Does superficial music dumb down the faith? Does our music nurture sensitivity to God? As Gaddy observes, "Worship strengthens a person's spiritual muscles. . . . And worship becomes better and better as worshipers become stronger and stronger."[23]

The point, evidently, is that the use of CWM made the contemporary congregation less responsible than the traditional congregation. Rather than nurturing them to maturity, it allowed them to remain self-indulgent.

Well, in the first place, if we want to be picky about it, Dawn's story tells us nothing about the relative maturity of the two congregations, only about the pastor's attitudes toward them.

But let us grant that the pastor's attitudes were appropriate. What conclusions follow?

It may have been that the selection of such a long scripture text was unwise. Perhaps the traditional congregation was willing to grit their teeth and bear it, because they knew that was what they were supposed to do, even though the long reading did not edify them. But the contemporary congregation might have been expected to object. Maybe the contemporary congregation is more to be commended in this particular instance. Surely we cannot assume that a scripture reading of *any* length is automatically an edifying experience and should be viewed with enthusiasm. If the pastor had chosen to read Psalm 119 in its entirety, doubtless many members even of the traditional congregation would have spoken to him about it after the service.

But let's assume further that the text in question was of reasonable, though somewhat unusual length, and that therefore the resistance of the contemporary congregation was a symptom of immaturity. Is it fair to claim that CWM was the cause, or even a cause, of that immaturity? I think not, without much more knowledge of the situation than Dawn supplies. Yes, of course, many of those who prefer CWM are immature. It is music of the young, and the young tend to be less mature than the old. But that's the whole point of CWM. CWM is Christian music that is immediately accessible—to the young as well as the old, to the immature as well as the mature. Therefore, as I have argued in chapter 5, it is an extremely valuable tool for teaching the immature, for helping the immature to become mature.

One could as easily say that children are immature because they sing songs like "The Wise Man Built His House Upon the Rock" and "Jesus Loves Me." (Cf. Dawn's metaphor about feeding kids a steady diet of candy.) But that is absurd. Children are immature because they are children. The genre of children's Christian music is intended, bit by bit, to instruct them and raise them out of their immaturity. For the sake of that task, it is better that children sing some children's hymns, rather than adult hymns alone. The same can be said of CWM.

There is truth in Gaddy's point that worship "strengthens our spiritual muscles," but it is certainly possible to take this principle too far. If a ten-minute Scripture reading strengthens our spiritual muscles, shouldn't a twenty-minute reading strengthen them even more? What about a reading that lasts an hour? two hours? Certainly, after a while, diminishing returns set in. As with physical exercise, a certain amount is beneficial, but too much can kill you. We shouldn't assume, therefore, as did some in the monastic tradition and as Dawn appears to assume here, that the best kind of worship is always that which is most unpleasant and punishing, that which presses hardest upon the comfort zone of the worshipers.

Indeed, Jesus' attitude is very different.

> Come to me, all you who are weary and burdened, and I will give you rest. Take my yoke upon you and learn from me, for I am gentle and humble in heart, and you will find rest for your souls. For my yoke is easy and my burden is light. (Matt. 11:28)

Our Lord was not saying, of course, that worship should always be maximally easy and comfortable. But Scripture certainly does not demand either that worship be made as unpleasant as possible. There are burdens to be borne in worship, but they are light.

The heaviness of worship is its challenge to our sin, which is relieved wonderfully and freely by God's grace. Biblical worship is not to be heavy in the sense of demanding instant appreciation for high culture, intellectual profundity, and endless readings.

But if we are to insist on some discomfort as a means of spiritual exercise in worship, shouldn't that burden be borne more equitably than Dawn prescribes? I believe that much of the pressure to keep traditional liturgy stems from, precisely, a desire for comfort. The question is, whose comfort? My wish is that all parties in the church would be more willing to sacrifice their comforts in order to love one another and to further the mission of the church.

At any rate, Dawn fails, finally, to convince me that CWM damages the character of worshipers. She does convince me that it is generally unwise to divide the congregation into traditional and contemporary. Certainly both groups need one another. And the experience of learning to appreciate one another's music is a valuable "spiritual exercise"!

And although I agree with Dawn that there are probably more mature Christians who prefer traditional hymns and more immature Christians who prefer CWM, I would insist that neither group is perfectly sanctified. My observation (if I too am entitled to nonspecific observations) is that in traditionalist circles there is too much pride, too much indifference to those outside of Christ, too much wanting to be comfortable with one's own preferred styles. That too is immaturity, and worship ought to deal with it.

Hunting Heresy in CWM

Dawn also criticizes the theological orthodoxy of CWM songs, rather to her own disadvantage, in my opinion. She offers only one example of a CWM song that she thinks is doctrinally unorthodox. Typically, she does not identify the author or give publication data, but the title appears to be "Mighty, Mighty Savior":

The chorus is

Mighty, mighty Savior, Mighty, mighty Lord,
Mighty, mighty Savior, You are my God. [Repeat.]

Then the verses are as follows:

> Father! Father! Father, my Lord.
> Father! Father! Father, my Lord. Let Your praises ring.
> Let Your people sing That you are a . . . [Chorus]

> Jesus! Jesus! Jesus, my Lord.
> [Continue as v. 1.]

> Spirit! Spirit! Spirit of God.
> [Continue as v. 1.][24]

She faults the song for not saying much and for calling each person of the Trinity a mighty Savior.

On the first point: the song does teach of (1) God's might, (2) his salvation, (3) his lordship, (4) his personal relation to us ("my" God, "my" Lord), (5) that God has a people, (6) that God's people should praise him, (6) that God is in three persons—Father, Jesus, and Spirit. Those truths are not negligible. That the song manages to present them in such conciseness and memorability is a considerable accomplishment.

Some may think that such a schema exaggerates the breadth of teaching in this song. Maybe so. Certainly this song doesn't "say much" compared to most traditional hymns. But what it says is important. It just focuses on a *few* important truths, rather than many at once. As we saw in chapter 5, CWM songs do not attempt to cover a great deal of doctrinal territory but to cover a small amount of teaching vividly and memorably. Doctrinal coverage is a luxury in the CWM repertoire. But these songs sometimes do present doctrine broadly as well as vividly.

Dawn's second point is that the song makes a doctrinal mistake by calling each member of the Trinity a "mighty savior." Well, we know that Jesus is called Savior in Scripture. But the term is also used more broadly. The book of Isaiah frequently refers to God as Savior without mentioning specifically any person of the Trinity (as 43:3, 11; 45:15, 21; 49:26; 60:16; 63:8). Certainly in the theology of the Bible all three persons are involved in the salvation of God's people. Generally, the Father plans, the Son accomplishes the Father's plan, the Spirit applies the finished work of the Son. Even to say that, of course, is to fall short of the *circumincessio*, the doctrine that each person is "in" the other two, so that all three persons are active in everything God does. So it would be very misleading theologically to insist, as Dawn appears to here, that salvation is the work of only one of the three persons. Thus it would seem to be the songwriter rather than Dawn who has the deeper grasp of biblical theology.

We should see that despite the rather broad statements often made about the doctrinal inadequacies of CWM, it is not easy to find an actual example of heresy. Indeed, CWM is pretty successful at insulating itself from false teaching, simply by sticking close to the scriptural text. My own view is that for this reason there is probably less heresy in CWM than there is in any other tradition of hymnody.

Narcissism?

Dawn tries to be balanced and friendly to both sides, but when I look closely at her arguments, it seems to me that she is often unfair. Over and over, she fails to take seriously the virtues of CWM or the possible dangers within the traditional styles of worship.

In chapter 3 of my book, I have drawn attention to the God-centeredness of CWM. One would think that critics devoted to fairness and committed to the theological standard of God-centered worship would take at least some pleasure in this remarkable fact. But instead, critics of CWM, with little if any hesitation, regularly identify CWM with what Christopher Lasch called "the culture of narcissism."[25] So Dawn says, evidently referring to CWM, that

> some worship planners and participants think that to praise God is simply to sing upbeat music; consequently, many songs that are called "praise" actually describe the feelings of the believer rather than the character of God.[26]

She gives no specific examples of this confusion. No doubt she is right to say that "some worship planners and participants" think this way; doubtless almost any conceivable error can be ascribed to some worship planners and participants. Dawn, however, evidently intends this as a serious criticism of the "contemporary worship" movement. But the standard texts of that movement, particularly of CWM, tell a different story. Of the songs listed in the MMPCB index under "adoration and worship," very few of them are upbeat, though some of them are. There is no evidence, certainly, of any confusion between praise and upbeat music.

Do praise songs express the feelings of the believer rather than the character of God, as Dawn claims? Well, of course, all song in worship, including the biblical Psalms, expresses to some extent the feelings of the believer. That is hardly ground for criticism.[27] But in CWM there is much reference to God's character, his attributes, his Trinitarian nature, and his mighty saving acts. One honestly wonders what praise songs Marva Dawn has been listening to.

At one point she does give an example. It is a song called "I Will Celebrate," which she heard at a denominational convention. There are two songs with that title in MMPCB (61 and 112); the one she cites is neither of those, but this, which I quote in part:

> I will celebrate, sing unto the Lord.
> I will sing to God a new song. [Repeat.]
>   I will praise God,
>   I will sing to God a new song. [Repeat.]
>   Hallelujah, hallelujah, etc.

She comments,

> God is never the subject in this song, but with all the repeats "I" is the subject 28 times! With that kind of focus, we might suppose that all the "Hallelujahs" are praising how good I am (without any *we* of community!) at celebrating and singing. I poke fun at this ditty because it is not immediately obvious that the song really does not

praise God at all. The words say *I will,* but in this song I don't, because, though God is mentioned as the recipient of my praise and singing, the song never says a single thing about or to God. If an unbeliever heard the words, she would have no idea of why God is praiseworthy or of who God is.[28]

In reply: (1) The song in question is primarily a declaration of one's intention to praise. Although it is possible linguistically to distinguish such a declaration from actual praise, the line between the two certainly blurs in actual worship. In Psalm 144, the psalmist sings "Praise be to the LORD my Rock" (v. 1). Does he stop praising God and start doing something else in verse 9 when he says "I will sing a new song unto you, O God"?

(2) Whether or not we want to press that distinction, it certainly is legitimate in worship both to praise and to declare one's intention to praise. The Psalms abound in such declarations (7:17; 9:1–2; 21:13; 22:22; 28:7, etc.),[29] and historic liturgies of the church have included them. So even if "I Will Celebrate" is merely a declaration of intention, rather than actual praise, it is not thereby unfit for worship. In that case, of course, it would have to be supplemented by other songs, which express "actual praise."

(3) The song is also, by its "Hallelujahs," an exhortation to others to praise, since *hallelujah* is a Hebrew imperative with "the Lord" as object, meaning "praise the Lord." One could make a point similar to Dawn's, saying that the song exhorts others to praise without actually expressing praise. But does anybody really believe that *hallelujah,* "praise the Lord," is a mere exhortation and not actual praise? This distinction, like Dawn's, breaks down in actual singing. But even granting it, would anybody seriously suggest that we exclude *hallelujah* from Christian worship? Psalmists in Scripture often exhort Israel to praise, and with this very word.[30]

(4) Dawn's supposition that the "Hallelujahs" are self-congratulatory is gratuitous and judgmental if she intends it to be taken seriously. If not, I do not find the remark amusing.

(5) The frequency of the pronoun "I" should also be compared

with the Psalms. In Psalm 18, it is used nineteen times, in Psalm 31, sixteen times. It is found frequently in many other psalms. Its frequency in "I Will Celebrate" seems relatively great, since Dawn counts all the repetitions. But if repetition is not a mortal sin, the number of "I's" in the song does not seem out of line. In any case, the idea that to use the pronoun "I" automatically detracts from God-centeredness is simply unbiblical. It pits the vertical focus against the horizontal (discussed in chap. 2).

(6) In the matters with which Dawn is concerned, this song is rather atypical of CWM. Most praise songs do speak about God and address praise specifically to him. About the service where she heard "I Will Celebrate," she says,

> Furthermore, in the rest of the service there was not one song that said anything about the God we were suppos-edly praising—all the songs were about us.[31]

Frankly that comment surprises me. If one flips randomly through MMPCB, one finds quite a lot of references to God's attributes and actions, many to his Trinitarian character. It is possible that some spiritually immature worship leader at the denominational conference excluded all hymns that said anything about God. It would, however, have required an almost diabolical ingenuity to steer clear of *any* reference to God at all in the CWM literature. Avoiding God in CWM is difficult, to put it mildly. And it is also possible that Dawn exaggerated the problem. Perhaps she was not paying very close attention.

There is evidence throughout her discussion that she has not paid close attention to CWM. She displays a lack of perspective remarkable for someone with her obvious gifts of intellect and scholarship. Does she really believe, on the basis of her experience, that CWM is *generally* narcissistic? If she does, then I can only con-clude that she doesn't know CWM. She misses what is most ob-vious about the genre and accuses it of narcissism on no good ground. She condemns the whole movement on the basis of one atypical example, and even that example does not deserve her con-demnation.

Fairness in Debate

On the other hand, Dawn devotes extraordinary energy toward finding virtues in traditional worship, supposedly not shared by CW or CWM. Like many liturgical theologians, for example, she gives to short liturgical sentences the highest recommendations while relegating CWM songs to the ash heap. She says,

> Many other pieces of a worship service can work to keep God the subject. I especially love the set of liturgical lines, "Glory to you, O Lord" and "Praise to you, O Christ," before and after the Gospel reading. The first line prepares our hearts and minds for the first climax of the service, the words and deeds of Jesus himself. While we sing this line with great gusto, we leap to our feet to exalt Christ and say, "You are honored, Lord! Come to us now and teach us. Tell us again what you have done for us. What a great gift that you come to us this way!" The second line recognizes that what we have just heard is life-changing because Christ, the Word, has met us in the Scripture that testifies of him. "You are worthy of praise, Christ, for you are indeed God in the flesh, and you have come to us in this revelation of truth for our lives." When such lines of the liturgy are well taught, the refrains open our minds to receive the Gospel as the presence of Jesus Christ. He is there to draw us to worship and thoroughly to change our lives by his Word.[32]

Remarkable how much meaning Dawn gets out of these two little sentences! That's fine with me. Certainly she is right to point out that in the proper context, with good teaching and preparation a short sentence can make a great impact upon a worshiper. I doubt if those sentences affect all worshipers the way they affect Marva Dawn, but I am happy to acknowledge them as worthy vehicles of God's Word and all its blessings.

But why should we not read CWM songs in the same way? If simple but scriptural sentences can make a powerful impact on the soul of a sophisticated theological writer, why shouldn't a CWM chorus, well placed in the service, also be, for all its simplicity, a source of rich blessing to the heart? Perhaps Dawn is giving the benefit of the doubt to her liturgical sentences, thinking more of what they could mean to worshipers than of what they usually do mean to them. But why should we not give a similar benefit of the doubt to CWM songs?

At another point in the book, Dawn says,

> Constant repetition of only one attribute of God can lead to profound reflection upon it, as in the gentle choruses from Taizé, but often endless repetitions are only boring failures to create fresh images revealing new aspects of the infinite God or presumptuous rejections of the multiplicity of images found in the Scriptures and in the Church's tradition. To sing over and over again only that God loves us is to miss the truth of God's wrath, the need for our repentance in light of God's justice, and God's mercy and truth in answer to the confusions of a broken and sinful world. Moreover, mindless refrains about God's love seldom include any elaboration, such as images to tell us how that love is manifested or how we know it.[33]

I have defended in this book the repetitiousness of many CWM songs. Here I find it interesting that Dawn commends the "gentle choruses from Taizé" which focus repetitiously on a single attribute of God, while condemning the repetitiousness of CWM. As I have indicated, it simply isn't true that CWM is full of mindless repetitions about love, and what repetition there is, is similar to that in Scripture itself. If Dawn had given to CWM the level of sympathetic consideration that she gives to the Taizé choruses, she would have commended the former.

I confess that I don't entirely understand how a writer who gets off to such a good start, offering a balanced, thoughtful perspective, can in the final analysis produce an argument that is quite unfair and not well informed about the objects of her criticism. Nevertheless, her book did encourage me to think through these issues more thoroughly, and I do recommend it to others for this purpose. The experience of interacting with this book taught me how difficult it is to see others the way they see themselves in controversies over worship. It is entirely likely that my own writing shows bias of the same kind. But to overcome that, we all need to be more aware of its pervasiveness in the discussion. That we can certainly learn from Dawn's book.

Notes

1. Grand Rapids: Eerdmans, 1995.
2. Marva Dawn, *Reaching Out,* 7. She cites Jane Healy's *Endangered Minds* (New York: Simon and Schuster, 1990).
3. Dawn, *Reaching Out,* 7.
4. Ibid.
5. Ibid., 3; cf. 169–70.
6. Ibid., 87.
7. Ibid., 93; cf. 58–60.
8. Ibid., 4. I agree emphatically with the main point. However, I think it odd that she finds the unnuanced "either/or" to be a product of modernity. Does everything bad have to be a product of modernity? Unnuanced either-or thinking has been a problem for many centuries. If anything, the modern (or "postmodern") period has become too intellectually squishy, so that there are actually too many "both/ands." One must examine the particular issue to determine whether it demands an either-or or a both-and response.
9. Ibid., 87, 166.
10. Ibid., 170.
11. In the text, I address the question of whether CWM is more prone to theological error than are other forms of hymnody.
12. Dawn, *Reaching Out,* 173–74.
13. Though perhaps it is "related to" it. Everything, after all, is related to everything else.
14. Dawn, *Reaching Out,* 172. She quotes Raymond T. Gawronski, "Why Orthodox Catholics Look to Zen," *New Oxford Review* 60 (July-Aug. 1993), 14.
15. MMPCB, 233.
16. Ibid., 217.
17. Ibid., 25.
18. Ibid., 243.
19. Ibid, 244.
20. Dawn, *Reaching Out,* 4.
21. Ibid., 167.
22. Ibid., 175.

23. Ibid., 176. She quotes C. Welton Gaddy, *The Gift of Worship* (Nashville: Broadman, 1992), 159.

24. Dawn, *Reaching Out*, 173.

25. See Christopher Lasch, *The Culture of Narcissism: American Life in an Age of Diminishing Expectations* (New York: W. W. Norton, 1979). There are many references to this book in Dawn's critique of modern evangelical worship (including CWM), as in David Wells's two books, *No Place for Truth, or Whatever Happened to Evangelical Theology?* (Grand Rapids: Eerdmans, 1993), and *God in the Wasteland: The Reality of Truth in a World of Fading Dreams* (Grand Rapids: Eerdmans, 1994), chief sources of Dawn's critique.

26. Dawn, *Reaching Out*, 87. For similar thoughts, see Michael Horton, *In the Face of God* (Dallas: Word, 1996), 200.

27. When Dawn (*Reaching Out*, 87) paraphrases Leander Keck in saying, "Praise does not express our own yearnings or wishes; it responds to something given to us," she makes an artificial distinction. To praise God is at the same time to affirm him and all his purposes, and to identify our own yearnings with his. To do that is to "respond to something given to us."

28. Ibid., 108. She lists no author or publication data for the song.

29. Dawn actually quotes Ps. 9:1 on 109!

30. The traditional doxology, "Praise God from Whom All Blessings Flow" is, technically, not praise, but an exhortation to praise. But does anyone suppose that in singing that song we are not actually praising God? We are singing that God is so great and wonderful (both in his providence, "from whom all blessings flow," and in his Trinitarian nature, "Father, Son, and Holy Ghost") that he deserves the praises of every creature in heaven and on earth. To sing that is to sing praise.

31. Dawn, *Reaching Out*, 108–9.

32. Ibid., 79.

33. Ibid., 89–90. The repetition in CWM has led some critics to describe them as "Christian mantras."

APPENDIX 2

❧

Sola Scriptura
in Theological Method

I have been motivated to write this book as much by concerns about the theological method lying behind criticisms of CWM as by concerns about the use of CWM itself. This essay, which doesn't mention CWM at all, indicates the methodological issues I have in mind. It is related to the CWM question in this way: In my opinion, the critics have frequently condemned CWM, not on the basis of biblical principle, but because they judge it to be part of a historical development of which they disapprove. That kind of argument seems to me to be unfair to CWM. More importantly for many other areas of discussion, it violates *sola Scriptura,* one of the defining principles of Protestant theology.

I hope that this book will be seen as a serious theological contribution to the discussion of worship, rather than one more airing of that emotion and prejudice which has so far dominated the discussion on both sides. I have written other books on matters of theological epistemology, and this one should be seen as a further development of those thoughts, rather than as a kind of holiday from academic theology. This appendix helps readers to understand some of the epistemological presuppositions underlying

175

the argument of the book, and the application of those particularly to the place of the intellect in worship, the use of tradition and confessions in the planning of worship, and the role to be played in our deliberations by the historical and sociological analysis of culture.

This article is also a very personal statement. It formulates concisely the central burden of my theological efforts in the past, and most likely also in future writings. It sets forth the direction in which I believe evangelical theology must go in order best to edify God's people and to penetrate the culture with the message of the gospel.[1]

In Defense of Something Close to Biblicism: Reflections on Sola Scriptura *in Theological Method*

My overall purpose in this essay is to reiterate the Reformation doctrine of *sola Scriptura,* the doctrine that Scripture alone gives us ultimate norms for doctrine and life, and to apply that doctrine to the work of theology itself, including both historical and systematic disciplines. That point may seem obvious to many of us, but I am convinced that certain applications of this doctrine need to be re-emphasized in the present situation.

Biblicism

The term "biblicism" is usually derogatory. It is commonly applied to (1) someone who has no appreciation for the importance of extrabiblical truth in theology, who denies the value of general or natural revelation, (2) those suspected of believing that Scripture is a "textbook" of science, or philosophy, politics, ethics, economics, aesthetics, church government, etc., (3) those who have no respect for confessions, creeds, and past theologians, who insist on ignoring these and going back to the Bible to build up their doctrinal formulations from scratch, (4) those who employ a "proof texting" method, rather than trying to see Scripture texts in their historical, cultural, logical, and literary contexts.

I wish to disavow biblicism in these senses. Nevertheless, I also want to indicate how difficult it is to draw the line between these biblicisms and an authentic Reformation doctrine of *sola Scriptura*. Consider, first, (1): *Sola Scriptura* is the doctrine that Scripture, and only Scripture, has the final word on everything, all our doctrine, and all our life. Thus it has the final word even on our interpretation of Scripture, even in our theological method.

It is common to draw a sharp line between the interpretation of Scripture and the use of Scripture to guide us in matters of philosophy, politics, economics, etc. This is sometimes described as a line between finding "meaning" and making "application." I have elsewhere given reasons for questioning the sharpness of this distinction.[2] For now let me simply point out that neither interpretation nor application is a mere reading of Scripture. In both cases, the scholar asks questions of the text and answers them using some scriptural and some extra-scriptural data. This activity takes place even at the most fundamental levels of Bible interpretation: the study of words and syntax, the work of translation, the attempt to paraphrase. So what we call "interpretation" is a species of application. In it, scholars ask their own questions of the text and apply the text to those questions. Questions of Bible interpretation and questions of, say, Christian political theory, are, of course, different in their subject matter, though there is some overlap. And the questions of interpretation certainly precede the questions of, for example, application to contemporary politics in any well-ordered study. Even so, sometimes our conclusions about politics present analogies applicable to other fields and therefore of broader hermeneutical significance. Thus conclusions about politics can in some ways be "prior to" hermeneutics as well as the other way around, illustrating further the broad circularity of the theological enterprise. But my main point here is that both types of study involve asking contemporary questions of the text, and thus they are usefully grouped together under the general category of application. In both types of cases we apply Scripture to extra-scriptural questions and data.

There is, therefore, an epistemological unity among all the different forms of Christian reflection. In all cases, we address extrascriptural data, and in all cases we consider that data under the *sola Scriptura* principle. That principle applies to Christian politics as much as to the doctrine of justification. In both cases, Scripture, and Scripture alone, provides the ultimate norms for our analysis and evaluation of the problematic data before us.

It is important both to distinguish and to recognize the important relations between Scripture itself and the extrascriptural data to which we seek to apply biblical principles. Scripture is something different from extrabiblical data. But what we know of the extrabiblical data, we know by scriptural principles, scriptural norms, the permission of Scripture. In one sense, then, all of our knowledge is scriptural knowledge. In everything we know, we know Scripture. To confess anything as true is to acknowledge a biblical requirement upon us. In that sense, although there is extrabiblical *data,* there is no extrabiblical *knowledge.* All knowledge is knowledge of what Scripture requires of us.

At this point, we may well be suspected of biblicism, for the biblicist, as we have seen, also disparages extrabiblical knowledge. But unlike the biblicist, we have recognized the importance of extrabiblical *data* in the work of theology and in all Christian reflection.

Which brings us to number 2 among the distinctives of biblicism: From a viewpoint governed by *sola Scriptura,* the "scope"[3] of Scripture, the range of subject matter to which it may be applied, is unlimited. As Cornelius Van Til says, there is a sense in which Scripture "speaks of everything":

> We do not mean that it speaks of football games, or atoms, etc., directly, but we do mean that it speaks of everything either directly or indirectly. It tells us not only of the Christ and his work but it also tells us who God is and whence the universe has come. It gives us a philosophy of history as well as history. Moreover, the information on

these subjects is woven into an inextricable whole. It is only if you reject the Bible as the Word of God that you can separate its so-called religious and moral instruction from what it says, e.g., about the physical universe.[4]

Here we hear Kuyper's claim that all areas of human thought and life must bow before the Word of God. We also begin to smell the odor of biblicism: Scripture speaks of football games, atoms, cosmology, philosophy. But there is a difference. Van Til is not saying that Scripture is a "textbook" of all these matters. Hence his distinction between "direct" and "indirect." Nor did Van Til deny, as biblicists have sometimes been accused of doing, that Scripture is a "centered" book. As a faithful disciple of Geerhardus Vos, he understood that Scripture is concerned to tell a particular "story," the story of God's redemption of his people through Jesus. The direct-indirect distinction should be taken to make this point as well: that Christ is central to the biblical message in a way that football games and atoms are not. But like the biblicist, Van Til believed that every human thought must be answerable to God's Word in Scripture. To many, this affirmation will sound biblicistic in the present context of theological discussion.

Distinctive 3 of biblicism raises the question of the relation between Scripture and the traditions of the church. *Sola Scriptura* historically has been a powerful housecleaning tool. By this principle the Reformers gained the freedom to question the deliverances of popes, synods, and councils, as well as those of learned and respected past theologians. They did respect tradition, particularly the early fathers and Augustine. But what was distinctive about the Reformation were its differences, rather than its continuities, with the past.

Certainly the Reformers did not, however, try to rebuild the faith from the ground up. They saw themselves as reforming, not rejecting, the teachings of their church. They saw the Protestant churches, not as new churches, but as the old church purified of works righteousness, sacerdotalism, papal tyranny, and the idolatry of the Mass. So they were not biblicists in sense 3. But they came close to it. In present-day Roman Catholic criticism of *sola Scriptura,* we are reminded of how close Protestantism does come to biblicism on this score.

Sola Scriptura actually provides support to theology against 4, the last kind of biblicism. For it places the *whole* Bible as authority over any specific exegetical proposal. Hence *Scriptura ipsius interpres.* This demands attention to contexts, narrow and remote. For an interpretation falsified by a relevant context is not an interpretation of *Scriptura.* Interpretations must also be consistent with what we know about the literary genres and historical backgrounds of the texts under consideration. Thus, as we saw under 1, we see that theology requires consideration of extrabiblical data. This is not so that we can be in line with secular fashions of thought. Quite the opposite: we do this to learn the true meaning of the Bible and thus to be accountable to it.

But for all this attention to contexts both scriptural and extrascriptural, *sola Scriptura* also demands that theological proposals be accountable to Scripture in a specific way. It is not enough for theologians to claim that an idea is biblical; they must be prepared to show in Scripture where that idea can be found. The idea may be based on a general principle rather than a specific text; but a principle is not general unless it is first particular, unless that principle can be shown to be exemplified in particular texts. So a theology worth its salt must always be prepared to show specifically where in Scripture its ideas come from. And showing that always boils down in the final analysis to citations of particular texts. This is why, for all that can be said about the abuses of proof texting, proof texts have played a large role in the history of Protestant thought. And there is something very right about that.

I conclude that although Protestant theology under the *sola Scriptura* principle is not biblicistic, it is not always easy to distinguish it from biblicism. We should expect that those who hold an authentic view of *sola Scriptura* will sometimes be confused with biblicists. Indeed, if we are not occasionally accused of biblicism, we should be concerned about the accuracy of our teaching in this area.

Sola Scriptura at Westminster Theological Seminary

Born out of the fundamentalist-modernist controversy, Westminster Theological Seminary (both eastern and western campuses) has always sought above all to deliver to its students "the whole counsel of God." It has remained firm on the doctrine of biblical inerrancy while other evangelicals have wavered, without falling into hermeneutical naiveté. The seminary has published four faculty symposia over its history, and all four of them have dealt in some way with biblical authority, sufficiency, and interpretation.[5]

Not only has the seminary taught an authentic Reformation theology of Scripture, but it has shown a particular zeal about teaching Scripture to its students. Westminster has emphasized the teaching of original biblical languages when such an emphasis has fallen into disfavor among evangelicals. It has provided very thorough instruction in the various parts of Scripture, and in the disciplines of exegetical, biblical, and systematic theology. In homiletics, it has stressed the use of biblical theology and in general the responsibility of the preacher to preach not himself but the Word. In apologetics and Christian philosophy it has continued Van Til's emphasis that Scripture has the right to rule every area of human thought and life.

But it is John Murray's view of method in systematic theology that I would consider at greater length. Murray taught at Westminster from 1930 to 1966 and left an indelible imprint upon the seminary. In his article, "Systematic Theology,"[6] Murray reviews the history of dogmatics, mentioning names such as Athanasius, Augustine, and Calvin.[7] He then comments,

> However epochal have been the advances made at certain periods and however great the contributions of particular men we may not suppose that theological construction ever reaches definitive finality. There is the danger of a stagnant traditionalism and we must be alert to this danger, on the one hand, as to that of discarding our historical moorings, on the other.[8]

He cites Calvin's own encounter with "stagnant traditionalism," when the Reformer dared to take issue with the view of Athanasius and others that the Son of God *"derived* his deity from the Father and that the Son was not therefore αυτοθεος."[9] He continues,

> When any generation is content to rely upon its theological heritage and refuses to explore for itself the riches of divine revelation, then declension is already under way and heterodoxy will be the lot of the succeeding generation. . . . A theology that does not build on the past ignores our debt to history and naively overlooks the fact that the present is conditioned by history. A theology that relies on the past evades the demands of the present.[10]

Murray here recognizes the importance of church history in the work of systematic theology, but he cautions us not to remain content with even the best formulations of past theologians. For the rest of the article, Murray drops the subject of historical theology entirely and focuses on the centrality of exegesis and biblical theology to the work of systematics.[11] Murray's actual theological writing consists almost entirely of the exegesis of particular texts: the proof texts of the doctrines under consideration.

There have been Reformed theologians (Berkouwer is the example that comes most readily to mind) who construct their theological writings as dialogue with past and contemporary theological texts. In these theologies, Scripture plays an important role, to be sure; but the exegesis is often somewhat sketchy and often seems like an addendum to the pages of historical analysis. Murray avoided that model of theology very self-consciously.

I remember many years ago helping to collate the results of a survey of Westminster alumni about the teaching they had received in seminary. One alumnus regretted that Westminster did not have any "real systematic theology." In his view, Murray's courses were not true systematics courses, but mere courses in exegesis. I disagree radically with that alumnus's evaluation of Murray, but I grant that that alumnus observed a genuine and important difference between Murray's teaching and other systematic theologians.

My own observation as a student was that Murray's approach was a wonderful breath of fresh air, despite his often opaque, archaic language and his insistence on the students' reproducing his lectures nearly verbatim on examinations. My fundamentalist friends at college criticized Reformed thinkers for relying on their traditions rather than the Bible. Murray showed me that the Reformed faith was purely and simply the teaching of Scripture. Thus he presented Reformed doctrine in the way most persuasive to Christian minds and hearts. This is the proper answer to anyone who considers Murray's method to be biblicist.

In short, a Westminster education trained students to ask first of all, about any subject matter whatever, what Scripture had to say about it. And it prepared students to expect Scripture to address every possible question in one way or another.

Westminster's Theological Creativity

The notion that Scripture addresses, to some extent, every important human question, produced at Westminster a high quality of theological creativity. We often associate orthodoxy with stagnancy and traditionalism. But at Westminster, the commitment to *sola Scriptura* propelled it in the opposite direction.

I have mentioned the independence of Murray's theology. He self-consciously followed the example of Calvin's struggle for the αυτοθεος: "A theology that relies on the past evades the demands of the present." And so Murray's theology impresses the reader both with its faithfulness to Scripture and with the independence and creativity of its formulations.

The same is even more obviously true with the thought of Cornelius Van Til: strongly insistent upon biblical authority and sufficiency; boldly innovative in epistemology and apologetics, and even in some theological formulations. Other examples, too, are not difficult to find, such as the redemptive-historical emphasis of Kuiper, Stonehouse, Clowney, Kline, and Gaffin, building on the work of Geerhardus Vos. I should mention also the nouthetic counseling of Jay Adams, building on the insight that Scripture has much to say about human problems, and that indeed it contains all of the ultimate norms for resolving them.

Even Westminster's teaching of church history has been creative. I remember Paul Woolley as a brilliant and urbane teacher, more like a Princeton professor than were any of his Westminster colleagues. We joked that Woolley was living proof that one need not have a Ph.D. to know everything. His independence of mind was legendary: in faculty meetings and church courts, he was often a minority of one, and it was rare that anybody could guess in advance on which side Woolley would come down. As a teacher, he had a rare ability (very much like that of J. Gresham Machen) to get inside the skins of historical figures whose ideas were very different from his own. Most of us emerged from his classes convinced that the Reformed way was best. But if we paid attention, we could not avoid a genuine sympathy for those in other traditions.

At times the creativity of Westminster has been problematic. Theonomy, for example, is certainly a child of Westminster. Its founder, Rousas J. Rushdoony, has seen himself as applying Van Til's insights to the areas of politics, economics, and social ethics. Both Gary North and the late Greg Bahnsen studied at Westminster. The two Westminster Seminaries have not been hospitable to theonomy,[12] but the movement has certainly introduced some new approaches in the use of Scripture and has challenged Reformed scholars to take more seriously the legal elements of God's Word.

I will not speak of Norman Shepherd's rethinking of the doctrine of justification, or of the "multi-perspectivalism" of Frame and Vern Poythress, concerning which different readers will have different opinions, except to say that in these cases as well, students of the early Westminster faculty were moved to reconsider traditional ideas by going back to Scripture. The important thing is that this creativity has not been at the expense of *sola Scriptura;* it has not been a movement away from Scripture to accommodate secular modes of thought, even though that is what "creativity" usually means in a theological context. Rather, as was the case with the first Protestant Reformers, it has been a creativity motivated by Scripture itself.

One might also raise questions concerning the relative absence at Westminster (again, I think mainly of the early 1960s when I was a student) of a confessional or traditional focus. I must be careful here in my formulation. But I felt as a student that we were being stimulated to originality more than we were being indoctrinated into a tradition. That may be a surprising comment, and I must immediately qualify it. All professors subscribed *ex animo* to the Westminster Confession and Catechisms, and the subscription formula was more detailed and forceful than most ordination vows in Presbyterian denominations. Our professors loved the great teachers of past ages: Augustine, Luther, Calvin, and the many others since their time. But Westminster was independent of denominational control, and students came from many denominational backgrounds, Reformed and non-Reformed. Students were not expected to subscribe to Reformed doctrine in order to matriculate or to graduate. There was, in my experience, an atmosphere of openness. We were encouraged to ask hard questions, and our professors generally sympathized with the questions, if not with our answers.

During my student years, I was never asked to read any of the Reformed confessions, or Calvin's *Institutes,* except in small bits. I never read any official standards of church government or discipline, not to mention Robert's Rules of Order. We used Hodge and Berkhof in our systematics classes, but for the most part we were graded not on our reading but on our knowledge of Murray's lectures. After graduation I became ordained in the Orthodox Presbyterian Church, and I confess I was rather surprised at the seriousness with which my fellow ministers took the confessional standards and Presbyterian traditions. Eventually I became more like my fellow Orthodox Presbyterian (and later Presbyterian Church in America) elders, but not without some nostalgia for the openness of theological discussion during my seminary years.

It is legitimate to criticize this openness in some respects. In my own theology courses, I always assign relevant portions of the confessions, and I try to make sure that every student understands the traditional formulations, even when I seek to improve upon them. Surely one important function of a seminary is to perpetuate and recommend the confessional traditions. Students seeking to be ordained in Reformed churches must understand fully what they are being asked to subscribe to. The Westminster of the early 1960s did not do a thorough enough job in that aspect of its teaching. I do believe it has improved since that time.

But as an academic theological community, seeking to encourage students how to do careful and hard thinking about theological issues, Westminster of the early 1960s was superb. I was not entirely ready for the Orthodox Presbyterian Church, but I was more than ready to do graduate study at Yale. Some students, I think, responded to this combination of freedom and orthodoxy in the wrong way: by taking the original insights of, say, Van Til, Kline, or Adams and trying to make them tests of orthodoxy.[13] But that was, I think, more the fault of the students than of the professors. Clearly, at any rate, Westminster's particular understanding of *sola Scriptura* led not to a stagnant traditionalism but to a flourishing of original and impressive theological thought.

Some Epistemological Observations

Westminster's use of *sola Scriptura* in theology is quite inescapable if we understand correctly the relationship between norm and fact in human knowledge. A description of church historical facts does not in itself tell us what we *ought* to believe. In and of itself, description does not determine prescription; "is" does not imply "ought." To suppose that it does has been called the "naturalistic fallacy." To assume that the historical genesis of an idea determines the proper evaluation of it is called the "genetic fallacy." To avoid these fallacies, our formulations of doctrines must always appeal to something beyond church history, to the biblical norm.

It is this insistence that distinguishes the Protestant *sola Scriptura* from the Roman Catholic view of tradition. And indeed, this principle itself is ultimately based on scriptural warrant. For Scripture itself condemns any appeal to tradition that places that tradition on the same level of authority as itself (Isa. 29:13; Matt. 15:8–9; Mark 7:6–7; Col. 2:22).

Sola Scriptura and Evangelical Intellectualism

Protestantism at its best has typically avoided opposing *sola Scriptura* to human reason as such. Reason is that God-given faculty which applies the norms of Scripture to the data of experience.[14] Therefore, the Reformers saw no conflict between *sola Scriptura* and high standards of scholarship. Luther and Calvin were scholars, and their theological distinctives were the result of careful scholarly exegesis. Indeed, in Protestantism to some extent even worship emulated the model of academic teaching. Ulrich Zwingli excluded music entirely from the worship of the church in Zurich, Switzerland, and made the church service into a teaching meeting. For this he has been accused of rationalism.[15] His policy was not followed by other Reformers, but there was among leaders of the Reformed churches a very cautious attitude about music. Following Book Three of Plato's *Republic,* they recognized a great emotional power in music, which could, if not tightly controlled, elicit unruly emotions and lead the worshipers away from the pure teaching of the Word. The early Reformed churches excluded musical instruments, and many excluded most hymns other than Psalm settings. There were theological reasons for these decisions,[16] but the net effect of them was to make worship much more an intellectual than an aesthetic experience.

Some Reformed scholars argued for the "primacy of the intellect," the doctrine that the intellect does or should rule unilaterally the will, emotions, and other aspects of human personality.[17] I reject this concept as well as the academic model of worship, and therefore I believe that Protestants have carried their intellectualism rather too far.

More serious, however, was the later modernist appeal to academic standards as a justification for the virtual abandonment of biblical authority. The theological modernists thought that a consistent respect for the intellect required them to accept the conclusions of the fashionable university scholarship. Protestantism affirms reason; why should it not accept the conclusions of recognized scholarship?

A proper answer to that question requires a distinction between the intellect itself and the norms that the intellect must follow in reaching its conclusions. Calvin affirmed the intellect, but he believed that the intellect should operate subject to the norms of God's Word. The modernists substituted for those norms the norms of secular scholarship, particularly the historical disciplines. As Van Til emphasized, the intellect, like a buzz saw, can function very well while pointing in the wrong direction. To make the right cut, the saw must not only turn efficiently; it must also be governed by a norm that points it the right way.

American evangelicalism inherited many of the ideas of the Reformers, but also many Anabaptist, Pietist, and Arminian influences. At times it produced notable scholarship, but it also went through some periods in which anti-intellectualism was dominant, particularly in the period following the infamous Scopes trial. Following the Second World War, however, Carl F. H. Henry, Harold John Ockenga, J. Howard Pew, Billy Graham, and others sought to lay foundations for a "new" evangelicalism, more hospitable to serious scholarship and compassionate social action. The new evangelical intellectuals, however, repeated the mistake of earlier Protestants by failing to face squarely the question of intellectual *norms*. They rejected the apologetic of Van Til, who insisted on the rule of Scripture in all human thought, and sought in various ways and degrees to find common ground with unbelief. I believe this uncritical intellectualism paved the way for the rejection of biblical inerrancy by many evangelicals in the 1960s. For many of them, a serious commitment to rationality demanded acceptance of the norms of critical biblical scholarship. Few even asked whether Scripture itself contained its own norms for scholarship, different from and opposed to those of the negative critics. So the sometimes sharp difference between evangelical and liberal scholarship has since the 1960s become a blur.

One breath of fresh air, however, during this period, came from Francis Schaeffer and his followers, such as Os Guinness, Udo Middelmann, Ranald Macaulay, and Jerram Barrs. They affirmed biblical inerrancy and insisted, like Schaeffer's teacher Van Til, that there was a sharp antithesis between those who believed in the biblical God and those who thought the universe was merely matter, motion, time, and chance. The latter position destroyed all meaning and intelligibility, they argued. They made their case learnedly and graciously, earning a wide readership and a position of respect, though not dominance, within evangelicalism.

These writers present a theology with real backbone, standing up courageously against secular thought and the secularizing movements within evangelicalism. But some unclarities remain. I cannot find in this literature any clear affirmation that Scripture contains its own distinctive epistemological norms, different from those of secular thought. Schaeffer, indeed, gave the impression that the secular philosophers of Greece affirmed an adequate concept of truth—"true truth" or "objective truth"—which was lost only in the wake of Hegel's dialecticism. And the Schaeffer apologetic focused to some extent upon "objective truth" as an abstraction, rather than that distinctive kind of truth, that divine Word, which is identical with Jesus himself. To that extent, the Schaeffer movement also has not been fully consistent with the Reformation *sola Scriptura*.

An Evangelical Critique of Culture

David Wells has expressed his debt to Francis Schaeffer, and the title of his *No Place for Truth* reminds us of Schaeffer's emphasis on "true truth." He reminds us of Schaeffer also in his conviction that the "modern" era is very different from previous times and therefore presents unique temptations to the church. Evangelicals, he thinks, have fallen prey to those temptations, to such an extent that God's truth no longer rules in the churches.[18]

In Wells's analysis, modernity has fostered a new way of thinking, which he characterizes in various ways, including the following:

1. Subjectivism: basing one's life upon human experience rather than upon objective truth.[19]

2. Psychological therapy as the way to deal with human needs.[20]

3. A preoccupation with "professionalism,"[21] especially business management and marketing techniques as the model for achieving any kind of common enterprise.[22]

4. Consumerism: the notion that we must always give people what they want or what they can be induced to buy.[23]

5. Pragmatism: the view that results are the ultimate justification for any idea or action.[24]

As I have noted in chapter 4, Wells sees this modern mentality as entirely detrimental to the church (thus his description of his book as "insistently antimodern"[25]). In the modern church, theology no longer rules.[26] God himself has becomes unimportant, "weightless."[27] His existence makes no difference to the church's practical decision making, says Wells. God is "user friendly," not the holy, transcendent, awesome God of Scripture.

Since theology no longer governs the church in any meaningful way,[28] sermons center on "felt needs," baptized equivalents of the latest cultural preoccupations, such as psychic well-being and success in marriage.[29] Church growth strategies and "megachurch" management and marketing theories replace biblical principle, so that congregations are viewed the same way businesses regard product consumers. As churches cater to people's wants instead of true spiritual needs, seminaries aspire to become professional schools, training ministers in these worldly values and skills.[30]

Wells's books are wonderfully erudite and eloquently written. And there is much truth, certainly, in his indictment of evangelicals as individuals and as churches. Some, however, have criticized his position as one-sided. Marva Dawn says,

> Wells's passion for truth needs to be balanced with an equally immense passion for love. He does indeed caution us appropriately to avoid an overly simplistic acceptance of technology that does not recognize the values of the attendant milieu. Moreover, he rightly bemoans the loss of biblical fidelity, which reduces the gospel's subversive power. However, his remarks do not seem to contain enough concern for how that truth can be communicated

to the modern generation, which has no context for receiving it. The Church needs careful creativity to find the best means for promulgating the truth and educative processes by which we can train the uninitiated in habits for cherishing it.

Unfortunately, many books that emphasize the pole of love within the dialectic discuss reaching the world outside the Church only in terms of marketing strategy.[31]

Dawn's comments raise the important question of *how* we can achieve such a balance in our critique of culture and of the church.

There is a remarkable irony about Wells's two books. On the one hand, his main theme is that theology should play a much larger role in the church's thinking, practice, evangelism, and worship. On the other hand, there is very little theology in either *No Place for Truth* or *God in the Wasteland*. There are a few theological observations, mostly about the transcendence of God, the importance of history, revelation, and eschatology.[32] But Wells's primary tools in these books are the disciplines of history and sociology. Through them, he discerns a process of change in American life over the last two hundred years, and he is able to trace changes in the church over the same period. Thus he is able to define the "modern" mentality and show how the church has capitulated to it.

What is the alternative? Here Wells does not go much beyond the negative point that we must reject the modern mentality. Although he does not quite say this, the structure of his argument strongly suggests that we ought to go back to the traditions of the church as they existed before the modern mentality took over. *No Place for Truth* begins with a very long discussion of the history of Wenham, Massachusetts: how it changed over two hundred years. He titles the chapter, nostalgically, "A Delicious Paradise Lost."[33] Doubtless he would not advocate that we merely turn back the clock. But the only guidance he gives us is that the old was better. Thus he gives aid and comfort to the most immovable traditionalists, and no help at all to the "reformers."

Or perhaps what he really wants us to do is to develop a strategy for present-day ministry by a "way of negation": whatever the modern marketers do, we should do the opposite. The Wellsian church would then become a mirror image of the marketer-consumer church, an exact reversal. But what is the opposite of consumerism? Giving no thought at all to the nature of the community to which one seeks to minister? Surely that is not what Wells would have us do. So mere negation is not much help. And as we know, mirror images retain many of the features of what they reflect. That should at least give us pause.

As Dawn says, there is imbalance in Wells's books. But the more fundamental problem is that of his *method*. A plea for the primacy of theology must itself, surely, be theologically grounded, not grounded merely in history or sociology. And surely our methods of evangelism and principles of worship must be based on Scripture, indeed *sola Scriptura*. Now of course scriptural principles must be applied to situations, and to understand the situation it is legitimate to consider data from history, sociology, and other sciences. But Scripture alone provides the ultimate norms for evaluating these data. So far as I can see, Wells never actually tries to formulate biblical principles of evangelism, church planting, or worship. Nor does he call our attention to other writings in which this work has been done. Rather, he oddly tries to derive these principles from his historical-sociological analysis itself, together with some broad concepts of divine transcendence and the like. Thus the reader is pushed toward either a blind traditionalism or a mirror-image reconstruction.

Simply opposing the modern model at every point is an entirely inadequate approach. I say that for *theological* reasons. I certainly wish to be counted among those whose thoughts and actions are based on principle, not pragmatism. But I confess I find myself, *on the basis of biblical principle itself,* very often siding with those who are considered pragmatists rather than with those who are regarded as the most principled among us.[34] The fact is that when we seriously turn to Scripture for guidance, that guidance usually turns out to be more complex, more nuanced, than anything we would come up with ourselves. Scriptural principle, typically, also leaves more room for freedom than man-made principles do, and, as we saw earlier, it gives more encouragement to our creativity. Certainly scriptural principle is more complex than any mere negation of existing cultural trends.

For one thing, Scripture itself does not merely negate the cultural trends of its time. It is true to say that in the Bible there is an antithesis between the wisdom of God and the wisdom of the world (1 Cor. 1–3), and between the church and the world (John 17:9–25; James 1:27; 4:4; 1 John 2:15–19). But Scripture never derives from this antithesis the conclusion that all our beliefs and actions must be opposite to those of the world. Unbelievers do know truth, although they suppress it (Rom. 1); so they can sometimes even teach God's truth with some accuracy (Matt. 23:1–4). And the church's missionaries must adopt at least some elements of the cultures they seek to reach with the gospel.[35] Says the apostle Paul,

> Though I am free and belong to no man, I make myself a slave to everyone, to win as many as possible. To the Jews I became like a Jew, to win the Jews. To those under the law I became like one under the law (though I myself am not under the law) so as to win those under the law. To those not having the law I became like one not having the law (though I am not free from God's law but am under Christ's law) so as to win those not having the law. To the weak, I became weak, to win the weak. I have become all things to all men so that by all possible means I might save some. (1 Cor. 9:19–22)

There are, in other words, some areas in which Christians may and should be like those to whom they preach, so that their witness may be more effective. Obvious instances are speaking the language of one's community and observing to some extent the local customs in food and clothing. The same principle, according to the above passage, applies to some kinds of moral scruples. For example, Paul may have observed the Mosaic dietary laws when in the company of Jews, but not when in the company of Gentiles.

This flexibility is not religious compromise. Paul did not disobey God when he behaved sometimes as a Jew, sometimes as a Gentile. It was God's own Word, indeed, that gave him the freedom to behave either way. This is not relativism. There were many areas where Paul did not have such freedom, many forms of worldly behavior that he plainly condemned (as in Gal. 5:19–21). But there were also significant areas of freedom. And Paul's judgments as to where he was free and where bound were based not on any autonomous analysis of culture but on the Word of God.

What about our own time? Does Scripture condemn all "marketing" techniques in setting forth the gospel? As we have seen in chapter 6, that depends on what you mean by marketing techniques. There are significant similarities between selling and preaching: Both activities convey information and seek to elicit a commitment. Both involve attracting the attention of an audience. To the extent that "marketing techniques" promote clear communication—vivid ways of drawing attention and motivating commitment—they are worthy of preachers' careful study.

Does that conflict with divine sovereignty? I think not. While God needs no human help to draw sinners to Jesus, he has freely chosen to use human means to accomplish this task in most cases (Matt. 28:18–20; Rom. 10:14–15; 1 Cor. 1:21). As in other aspects of salvation, there is in evangelism both divine sovereignty and human responsibility. We are responsible to preach and teach.

But to do that requires effort. We must speak clearly and persuasively in order to reproduce the clarity and persuasiveness of the gospel itself. That means learning rules for gospel communication just as a seller learns techniques for communicating the virtues of his product. Many of those techniques are valid for all forms of communication. So it is not impossible to imagine that we might learn something of value from secular marketing theorists.

Of course, there are many differences between evangelism and marketing. Because the church's "product" is eternally urgent—our ultimate need—our communication of it should reflect the solemnity and holiness of our God. It should reflect our own willingness to humble ourselves in order to exalt the Lord. In these respects, we leave the secular marketing world far behind.[36]

Sometimes, then, we can learn from the marketers, sometimes not. When they speak of the effects of filling an auditorium beyond 80 percent of its capacity, we do well to listen. Scripture never says that we must fill our buildings to the point of standing room before going to two Sunday morning services or two assemblies or a larger facility. But if marketers tell us we must avoid the subject of sin in order to attract seekers, we must disagree in the sharpest terms, for then biblical principle is at stake.

Likewise, is it wrong for preachers to address "felt needs" in preaching the gospel? We noted in chapter 6 that many felt needs today are genuine spiritual needs according to Scripture. People want to know how to make marriages work; the Bible answers that need (Eph. 5:22–33). People want to know how to avoid anxiety; Scripture addresses that concern too (Phil. 4:6–7). Why should preachers not address these topics in light of the riches of the gospel of Jesus Christ? Of course, many other felt needs (the "need" for health, wealth, self-esteem, etc.) are either ambiguous or condemned by Scripture. Nevertheless, even these subjects, when evaluated scripturally, should be addressed in preaching.

So biblical worship and evangelism should not be viewed as simple negations of every element of an unbelieving culture. Rather, there should be a discerning use of the elements of culture, governed by the values of God's Word.

Consider also the content of the church's preaching. Should it focus on the objective rather than the subjective, on God and history rather than our response, on objective truth rather than human experience, as Wells argues? Here I tend to be more sympathetic with Wells than I have been in the preceding paragraphs. I do believe that in general preaching today needs to place a greater emphasis on the objective.

But again Wells misses nuances. All knowledge involves both an object (what one knows) and a subject (the knower): you don't have knowledge unless you have both.[37] Scripture records the objective truth of God and redemption in connection with the experiences by which the biblical writers came to know these objective facts. Indeed there is in Scripture much teaching about believing subjectivity. The Psalms are full of the pronouns "I" and "we," as well as personal testimonies about how God has entered human experience. Scripture pays great attention to our emotional life: our joy, fear, anxiety, peace, anger, erotic passion, and so on.

As we have seen in chapter 8, there is a subjective side to salvation itself. The objective side is that Christ, the Son of God, lived a perfect human life, died for the sins of his people, rose from the dead and ascended into heaven. The subjective side is that when he died for sin, we died to sin (Rom. 6:1–14) and rose with Christ to newness of life. God not only atones, he regenerates. We are new creatures (2 Cor. 5:17), partakers of Christ's abundant life (John 10:10).

Preaching, in Scripture, does not merely present the objective truths of the history of redemption. It also responds to those truths in a personal way, giving testimony of what God has done in the life of the preacher and what he can do in the lives of the hearers. The Psalms are full of such testimony, as are the letters and sermons of Paul. And biblical preaching calls for its hearers to respond to it, both inwardly and outwardly. Biblical repentance is a change of heart that brings change in behavior, and it is a crucial goal of preaching (Acts 2:38–39).

Wells, therefore, loses credibility when he bases so much of his case on historical and sociological analysis, without giving substantial attention to the biblical values that must judge the culture. For one thing, our time is probably not much better or worse than past ages, contrary to Wells's Schaefferian rhetoric about the uniqueness of modernity. But in any case, we are to address culture today in the same way Paul addressed the culture of the first century: by the Word of God, communicated by all scripturally legitimate means available in the culture.

Confessionalism

The recent Cambridge Declaration of the Alliance of Confessing Evangelicals[38] seeks to recommend to the evangelical churches a renewed confessionalism. It is organized around the great *solas* of the Protestant Reformation: Scripture, Christ, grace, faith, and glory to God. Many emphases of this document are welcome and greatly needed. Naturally I am pleased that the first article reaffirms *sola Scriptura* and follows the sentence, "These truths we affirm not because of their role in our traditions, but because we believe that they are central to the Bible."

The document is recognizably Wellsian. In the *sola Scriptura* section, we read, "Therapeutic technique, marketing strategies, and the beat of the entertainment world often have far more to say about what the church wants, how it functions and what it offers, than does the Word of God." The discussion goes on to say that in these and other areas to which Wells has given attention, the church should turn to Scripture, rather than the culture, for its message. True enough. But as in Wells's books, I believe that more needs to be said. The attempt of churches to learn from therapists, marketers, and consumers is not, in my mind, motivated by unbelief pure and simple. If lack of faith is one factor, there is also the motive of seeking to reach out to the world, to apply scriptural principles in a way that is relevant to the present world and communicable to the unchurched. The strengths and weaknesses of this document are similar, then, to the strengths and weaknesses of Wells's own writings.

Positively, the document recommends a return to the attitudes and convictions of an earlier time.

> The faithfulness of the evangelical church in the past contrasts sharply with its unfaithfulness in the present. Earlier in this century, evangelical churches sustained a remarkable missionary endeavor, and built many religious institutions to serve the cause of biblical truth and Christ's kingdom. That was a time when Christian behavior and expectations were markedly different from those in the culture. Today they often are not. The evangelical world today is losing its biblical fidelity, moral compass and missionary zeal.[39]

The last sentence is surely true, but the rest of the paragraph seems rather naive in its assessment of evangelical Christianity in the early twentieth century. The missionary movement of those days was a wonderful thing in many ways, but as it was aided and abetted by the imperialism of the Western nations, it was not entirely counter-cultural, or unambiguously righteous. The document, like Wells's books, calls us back to a nostalgia for a past age. That, in my view, is a frail reed. It also calls us back to a greater fidelity to Scripture. That is a strong element in the document. But it needs to be spelled out in detail: what does Scripture say about missions, church growth, marketing, as opposed to the notions prevalent in our culture today? We need a document that gives us positive guidance, rather than merely negating present trends.

I certainly favor a renewed confessionalism if it means a better appreciation for the teaching of the Reformation *solas*, indeed for the distinctive teachings of the Reformed faith. The argument of this essay, however, should help us to guard against certain abuses of the confessionalist position, such as (1) emphasizing confessions and traditions as if they were equal to Scripture in authority, (2) equating *sola Scriptura* with acceptance of confessional traditions,[40] (3) automatic suspicion of any ideas from sources outside the tradition, (4) focusing on historical polemics rather than the dangers of the present day, (5) emphasizing differences with other confessional traditions to the virtual exclusion of recognizing commonalities,[41] (6) failing to encourage self-criticism within our particular denominational, theological, and confessional communities.

A reaffirmation of confessionalism for our time ought to repudiate the commonly understood equation between confessionalism and traditionalism. It should rather reiterate a doctrine of *sola Scriptura* like that of Westminster at its best: one that will encourage careful thinking about the movements of our time rather than overstated condemnations, one that will discourage romantic notions about past ages. A doctrine of *sola Scriptura* must actually, practically, point us not simply to generalizations about historical trends, but to Scripture itself for our standards.

Conclusions

In a number of ways we can improve on Wells's analysis by a more consistent application of *sola Scriptura:* We can see more fully the ways in which modern culture has strayed from God's path but also understand how to use certain elements of that culture with God's blessing. *Sola Scriptura*, which is often perceived as a narrowing, limiting doctrine, actually opens our vision to behold a greater complexity in modern culture than we would otherwise recognize. It is a *liberating* doctrine in the sense that it gives us greater freedom than any mere traditionalism or *via negationis* could provide. At the same time, it sets forth true restrictions on the use of culture with greater clarity and gives us direction to avoid the traps of the modernists and the evangelical accommodationists.

Westminster's emphasis on *sola Scriptura*, therefore, provides us with a powerful tool for the critical analysis of culture, one rarely found elsewhere in evangelical scholarship. It guards us against both secularism and traditionalism. We would be wise to continually stress this principle, neither compromising it nor forgetting to apply it to every matter of controversy.

Scripture, therefore, must be primary in relation to history, sociology, or any other science. It is Scripture that supplies the norms of these sciences and that governs their proper starting points, methods, and conclusions.[42]

Notes

1. This essay, in a slightly longer form, has been accepted for publication in the *Westminster Theological Journal*, together with replies by David Wells and Richard Muller, and a further response from me.

2. Frame, *Doctrine of the Knowledge of God* (Phillipsburg, N.J.: Presbyterian and Reformed, 1987), 81–85, 93–98, 140.

3. Or *scopus*, if you prefer.

4. Cornelius Van Til, *The Defense of the Faith* (Philadelphia: Presbyterian and Reformed, 1963), 8.

5. Paul Woolley and Ned B. Stonehouse, ed., *The Infallible Word* (Philadelphia: Presbyterian and Reformed, 1946; 3d rev. ed., 1967); John H. Skilton, ed., *Scripture and Confession* (Philadelphia: Presbyterian and Reformed, 1973); Harvie M. Conn, ed., *Inerrancy and Hermeneutic* (Grand Rapids: Baker, 1988); William S. Barker and W. Robert Godfrey, eds., *Theonomy: A Reformed Critique* (Grand Rapids: Zondervan, 1990).

6. In *Collected Writings of John Murray,* (Edinburgh: Banner of Truth, 1982), 4:1–21.

7. Ibid., 5.

8. Ibid., 7–8.

9. Ibid., 8.

10. Ibid., 8–9.

11. Compare B. B. Warfield, who in "The Idea of Systematic Theology," *Studies in Theology* (Oxford University Press, 1932; Grand Rapids: Baker, 1981), spoke of the relationship of systematics to historical theology as "far less close" than its relation to exegetical theology (p. 65). Note also his remarks about tradition on page 101.

12. See Barker and Godfrey, eds., *Theonomy.*

13. Cf. my observations on the "movement mentality" among some of Van Til's followers in my *Cornelius Van Til: An Analysis of His Thought* (Phillipsburg: Presbyterian and Reformed, 1995), 8–14, 17–18, passim.

14. I am not here defining reason, but rather describing one of its important functions in theology.

15. See Klass Runia, "The Reformed Liturgy in the Dutch Tradition," in Donald A. Carson, ed., *Worship: Adoration and Action* (Grand Rapids: Baker, 1993), 99, and Carlos M. N. Eire, *War Against the Idols* (Cambridge: Cambridge University Press, 1988).

16. Reasons that I have discussed and rejected in *Worship in Spirit and Truth* (Phillipsburg: P&R Publishing, 1996), chap. 11.

17. I have criticized this notion in Clark and Van Til in my *Cornelius Van Til,* 141–49.

18. Compare Schaeffer's alarms about the "Great Evangelical Disaster," in his book of that title (Westchester, Ill.: Crossway Books, 1981). To him, the disaster was particularly the evangelical compromise of biblical inerrancy. The focus of Wells's attention is somewhat different.

19. David Wells, *No Place for Truth* (Grand Rapids: Eerdmans, 1993), 118, 142, 172, 174, 264, 268, 278, 280, and many other places; *God in the Wasteland* (Grand Rapids: Eerdmans, 1994), 101–11.

20. *God in the Wasteland,* 61, 77–84, 115, 153, 176, 202.

21. *No Place for Truth,* 218–57.

22. Ibid., 60–87.

23. Ibid., 63–87, 100.

24. Ibid., 67.

25. *No Place for Truth,* 11.

26. Ibid., 218–57.

27. *God in the Wasteland,* 88–117.

28. *No Place for Truth,* 95–136; *God in the Wasteland,* 186–213.

29. *No Place for Truth,* 250–57; *God in the Wasteland,* 149–51.

30. *No Place for Truth,* 113–15.

31. Marva Dawn, *Reaching Out Without Dumbing Down* (Grand Rapids: Eerdmans, 1995) 60–61.

32. *No Place for Truth*, 270–82; *God in the Wasteland*, 118–85.

33. *No Place for Truth*, 17–52.

34. We may recall that Jesus himself was considered something of a pragmatist compared to the Pharisees, who proclaimed their allegiance to divine principle but in fact placed their tradition above God's Word. See, for example, Matt. 15:1–9.

35. For a full discussion of "antithesis," see my *Cornelius Van Til*, chap. 15.

36. Although this sort of self-abasing servant attitude deserves to be a model for Christians even in the marketing field!

37. And also, third, a norm or standard. See my *Doctrine of the Knowledge of God*.

38. I am working from a photocopied version without publication data.

39. Cambridge Declaration, 5.

40. Actually, as I have argued, it would be more accurate to derive from this principle a critical stance toward traditions.

41. For more observations on this subject, see my *Evangelical Reunion* (Grand Rapids: Baker, 1991), now out of print.

42. This essay will serve as my reply to Richard Muller's "'The Study of Theology' Revisited: A Response to John Frame," *Westminster Theological Journal* 56 (fall 1994), 409–17. I have not engaged Muller's arguments specifically, but, then, he did not engage mine either. But his response leaves me still with the impression that his theological method, in order to avoid some aspects of hermeneutical circularity, gives priority to neutral or autonomous historical study over the methodological principles of Scripture itself.

Index of Scripture

Index of Songs

(This index includes both traditional and contemporary songs cited in this book. See also the list of contemporary songs in chapter 12.)

Index of Names

John M. Frame (B.D., Westminster Theological Seminary; A.M. and M.Phil., Yale University) is professor of systematic theology and philosophy at Reformed Theological Seminary, Orlando campus. Noted for his works in theology, apologetics, and ethics, he is also a classically trained musician, an experienced worship leader in both traditional and nontraditional settings, and author of *Worship in Spirit and Truth.*